PRESENTED TO

_____

BY

_____

ON THE OCCASION OF

_____

_____

ON THIS DAY

_____

PROVERBS FOR KIDS FROM

THE BOOK

WITH THE 'VERBS

 Tyndale House Publishers, Inc.
Wheaton, Illinois

Scripture quotations are taken from *The Living Bible*. Scriptures compiled and arranged by Richard Osborne. Illustrations by Chris Kielesinski and Terry VanRoon.

'Verbs Copyright 1985, Impartation Idea, Inc.

First printing, October 1987
Library of Congress Catalog Card Number 87-50512
ISBN 0-8423-4975-8
Copyright 1987 by Tyndale House Publishers, Inc.
Printed in the United States of America

CONTENTS

THE TEACHING OF PROVERBS

PART ONE
GOD

PART TWO
BUILDING BLOCKS

PART THREE
LEARN AND DO

PART FOUR
BEAUTIFUL INSIDE

PART FIVE
DEPENDABILITY

PART SIX
SPEAKING THE TRUTH

PART SEVEN
HOME AND FAMILY

PART EIGHT
FRIENDS AND NEIGHBORS

PART THIRTEEN
YOUR BODY

PART FOURTEEN
THE GOOD LIFE

PART FIFTEEN
YOUR FUTURE

PART SIXTEEN
WORK AND MONEY

PART SEVENTEEN
TEACHING

PART EIGHTEEN
AND OTHER THINGS

INTRODUCING THE 'VERBS

The 'verbs were created to put the basic themes of Proverbs into action in a humorous and easy-to-learn way, with each of the non-human characters representing an element or attitude found in this ageless manual for daily life.

Joy and Smiley
They represent those who are searching for wisdom and trying to act accordingly.

Mr. Wisdom
He represents wisdom and is ready to teach all who will hear him.

Big and Bigger
They represent rewards and consequences by administering the results of good and bad actions.

B.A.
(Bad Attitude)
He represents those who reject wisdom. He's unteachable and always does things his own way.

JUST WHAT IS "WISDOM"?

The book you are holding in your hands is a book of wise sayings. You may be wondering what *wise* really is. What does it mean to be a wise person? The words *wise* and *wisdom* are found many times in the Bible, but many people are not sure just what a wise person is.

For the men who wrote the Bible, wisdom meant much more than just knowing facts. You go to school to learn facts about science, math, history, and literature, but knowing the facts does not mean you are wise. You can know a lot of things but still not get along well with people or act the way you should. To be wise means you know something about what God is like and can apply what you know to your daily life. In other words, it means you understand God, and your understanding leads you to obey God as you should.

The Book of Proverbs was written by men who knew a lot about God from their own experience and the experiences of other people. They understood that God is a loving Father who wants what is best for his children and who gives them principles to live by. They understood that things that seem so important to us—having money, being famous, knowing a lot of things—are not really as important as understanding God and letting him guide us. And they knew that having a truly successful life means living as if God were watching all our actions.

God himself is the source of wisdom. In the Old Testament many kings and leaders sought wisdom so they could rule better. King Solomon was one king who was especially famous for being wise. Like other men who were famous for their wisdom, he understood that God gives the ability to see the world and ourselves as we really are. Human ability is amazing, and scientists can discover many things without asking God for help. But real wisdom—real understanding of how we are to live our lives—comes only to people who love God.

People who love God know that he wants us to get along well with our friends and family. He wants us to be unselfish and kind, and he wants us to think carefully before we do things we may be sorry for later. Because he wants us to live happy, healthy lives, he gives wisdom.

You don't have to be a brilliant person to be wise. You only have to have the right attitude toward God. When you understand that God is in control of the world, you are on your way to being wise. When you let your love for God affect how you act toward your friends and parents, you are becoming wise. When you read books like Proverbs to learn more about how to live a good life, you are growing in wisdom. This book is designed to help you grow.

WHO SOLOMON WAS

Most of the Book of Proverbs was written by King Solomon. Solomon, son of King David of Israel, had a reputation for being a wise man. Early in his reign as king he was asked to serve as judge in a famous case that proved his wisdom. Two women both claimed to be the mother of the same child. Solomon ordered that the baby be cut in two, with half given to each woman. He knew that the real mother would never allow this, and, sure enough, the baby's real mother asked that the baby be given to the other woman. Solomon knew that this compassionate woman was the true mother, so she got the baby. The people of Israel knew from this ruling that their king was a shrewd judge of human nature. (This story is found in the Bible in 1 Kings 3:16-28.)

Solomon owed his wisdom to God. At the time he became king he had asked God to give him wisdom to govern the people of Israel. God was pleased that Solomon had asked for wisdom—and not for wealth or the destruction of enemies—and he gave Solomon what he asked for. In fact, God gave Solomon, who put wisdom above everything else, much more. He gave him riches and fame.

Kings in the ancient world often compiled collections of their wise sayings. Kings of Egypt and Arabia had been famous for their knowledge about how to deal with human affairs. But Solomon outdid them all. According to his story in 1 Kings, he spoke three thousand proverbs. Many of these are found in the Book of Proverbs. He also wrote the Book of Ecclesiastes and the Song of Solomon. Men of all nations came to hear Solomon's wisdom, and he was wise about almost everything. The queen of the faraway country of Sheba came to Israel and was amazed at how much

Solomon knew. He not only taught about the ways of God and man, but he also taught about plant and animal life.

Because Solomon was a wise ruler, the kingdom prospered during his reign. Israel was a larger country than it had ever been, and there were almost no wars during that time. Solomon directed the building of a magnificent temple in Jerusalem, a temple with beautiful furnishings of gold and bronze. His life is an example of something he taught in the Book of Proverbs: Those who seek wisdom from God also receive other blessings.

The wise king did not always act wisely. He angered God by marrying many foreign women, some of whom led him to worship other gods. God's punishment was the splitting of the kingdom into two separate kingdoms. But this did not occur until after Solomon's death. He died after reigning for forty years.

No one in Israel's history has a greater reputation for wisdom than Solomon. We are fortunate that the sayings of this wise king are available for us to learn from today.

PART ONE

GOD

TRUSTING GOD

f you want approval from both God and man, and a
reputation for good judgment, common sense, and
wisdom, then trust the Lord completely. Trusting God
also leads to prosperity, happiness, and safety. And those
who do will flourish like a tree. Those who trust in themselves
and are sure of their own wisdom are conceited. Ask the
Lord for the things you want. Don't trust in your money or
your own abilities or down you'll go. And trusting men for
answers is another dangerous trap. Disaster strikes like a
cyclone and the wicked are whirled away. But those who
trust God have a strong anchor.

Since the Lord is directing your steps, you need to trust
him. Why try to understand everything that happens along
the way? You can prepare yourself for the future, but remember that victory comes from God.

*Proverbs 1:7 / 3:4, 5, 7, 8 / 10:25 / 11:28 / 16:20 / 20:22, 24 / 21:31 / 22:17-19 / 24:10 /
28:25, 26 / 29:25, 26*

KNOWING GOD

Where there is ignorance of God and his laws, people get out of control. But knowing God is a wonderful thing. The people who know him end up with every other kind of understanding. So search for him as you would for lost money or hidden treasure; then the knowledge of God himself will be given to you.

Proverbs 2:3-5 / 9:10 / 29:18

REVERENCE FOR GOD

Blessed is the man who respects God and worships him. The man who doesn't care is headed for serious trouble, for the reverence and fear of God are basic to all wisdom. If anyone respects and fears God, he will hate evil and turn his back on it. Then he will be given renewed health and vitality, happiness, protection, and a long life. This man will be both wise and honored. Reverence for God is a fountain of life; its waters give a man deep strength and keep him from death. Continue to honor the Lord all the time, for surely you have a wonderful future ahead of you.

Proverbs 1:7-9 / 2:5 / 3:7, 8 / 8:13 / 9:10 / 10:27 / 14:26, 27 / 15:16, 33 / 16:6 / 19:23 / 22:4 / 23:17, 18 / 28:14 / 31:30

GOD'S WORD

Despise God's Word and you will find yourself in trouble. A man is a fool to trust himself, and only a simpleton believes everything he is told. A sensible man checks God's Word for wisdom and is safe. It is a treasure of knowledge and understanding. Every word proves true. Obey these words and you will make the right decision every time. Guard them as your most precious possession. Keep them deep within your heart. Then wisdom and truth will enter the very center of your being, filling your life with joy.

Proverbs 2:6-10 / 7:1-3 / 8:9 / 13:13 / 14:15 / 28:26 / 30:5, 6

PUT GOD FIRST

In everything you do, put God first, and he will direct you and crown your efforts with success. When you put God and what pleases him first, God makes even your worst enemies to be at peace with you. One way of putting God first is by giving him the first part of all your income. When you do this, he will cause all that you do to prosper.

Proverbs 3:6, 9, 10 / 9:10 / 16:7

WISDOM IN CREATION

The Lord's wisdom founded the earth; his understanding established all the universe and space.

"I am wisdom and I lived before the oceans were created, before the springs bubbled forth their waters onto the earth, before the mountains and hills were made. Yes, I was born before God made the earth and fields and the first handfuls of soil. I was there when he established the heavens and formed the great springs in the depths of the oceans. I was there when he set the limits of the seas and gave them his instructions not to spread beyond their boundaries. I was there when he made the blueprint for the earth and oceans. I was the craftsman at his side. I was his constant delight, rejoicing always in his presence. And how happy I was with what he created—his wide world and all his family of mankind. So, listen to me. For if God used wisdom to create the universe, shouldn't you use wisdom to shape your life?"

Proverbs 3:19, 20 / 8:22-32 / 16:4 / 30:1-4

GOD IS WITH YOU

The Lord is with you. You can live and sleep without fear, for he protects you. The Lord is watching everywhere and keeps his eye on both the evil and the good. But for the godly he is a strong fortress. Rely on him and you'll always be safe.

Proverbs 3:24-26 / 15:3 / 18:10 / 21:31

GOD'S BLESSINGS

The Lord's blessing is our greatest wealth. All our work adds nothing to it! Those who work hard to become rich but don't have God's blessing are actually poor. But if we have God's blessing, we are rich even if we are poor. God will cover the good and upright with blessings from head to foot. And those who trust and obey the Lord will be happy and never lose them. But the curse of God is on the wicked. They inwardly curse their luck and eventually they lose everything. Blessed is the man who reveres God, but the man who doesn't care is headed for serious trouble.

Proverbs 3:33 / 10:6, 22, 30 / 12:2 / 13:7 / 16:20 / 18:22 / 28:14

GOD SEES EVERYTHING

The Lord is watching everywhere and keeps his eye on both the evil and the good. Even the depths of hell are open to God's knowledge. How much more the hearts of all mankind!

Proverbs 5:21 / 15:3, 11, 29 / 20:27 / 24:11, 12

PLEASING GOD

Many favors are showered on those who please God. The way to please God is by being wise. He is also pleased when you are just and fair. When you are trying to please God, God makes even your worst enemies to be at peace with you. God's anger is as dangerous as a lion's. But his approval is as refreshing as the dew on grass.

Here are four things that honor God:

- giving him the first part of all your income,
- doing right,
- helping the poor,
- being a sensible son or daughter.

Proverbs 3:9, 10 / 8:35 / 14:2, 31 / 16:7, 15 / 19:12 / 21:3 / 27:11

PRAYER

The Lord is far from the wicked, but he hears the prayers of the righteous. Every promise of God proves true. He helps all who come to him and ask. God also helps others when you pray for them. And he is pleased when you pray for those who are unkind to you. God doesn't listen to the prayers of those who break the law, but he delights in the prayers of his people. If you want something, don't try to get it without God's help. Ask him for it.

Proverbs 15:8, 29 / 28:9 / 29:10, 26 / 30:5

28

GOD'S PRINCIPLES

The Lord demands that things be done according to his Word. His Word shows us how to act and what to do. These instructions are God's established principles. It is selfish to quarrel against these principles by demanding your own way. But if you do, don't blame God for your failure. You've ruined your chances by your own foolishness.

Proverbs 16:11 / 18:1 / 19:3

LIGHT

Everyone depends on God for light. The good man's life is full of light. But the light of the wicked will be snuffed out. God also puts out the light of anyone who curses their father or mother. Yes, the sinner's road is dark and gloomy. So don't envy the wicked, for there is no future in darkness. If a wicked person tries to deceive you, don't believe him. Stay in the light and the darkness in their hearts will be exposed for all to see.

Proverbs 13:9 / 20:20 / 24:19, 20 / 26:24-26 / 29:13

PART TWO
BUILDING BLOCKS

WISDOM

"I wisdom, give good advice and common sense. Because of my strength, kings reign in power, and rulers make just laws. I love all who love me. Those who search for me shall surely find me. Unending riches, honor, justice, and righteousness are mine to distribute. My gifts are better than the purest gold or sterling silver! My paths are those of justice and righteousness. Those who love and follow me are indeed wealthy. I fill their treasuries. How happy are all who follow my instructions. Listen to my advice—oh, don't refuse it—and be wise. For whoever finds me finds life and wins approval from the Lord. But those who miss me have injured themselves irreparably. Those who refuse me show that they love death."

Proverbs 8

32

INSIGHT AND DISCERNMENT

Yes, if you want better insight and discernment, and are searching for them as you would for lost money or hidden treasure, then they will be given to you. God will show you how to distinguish right from wrong and how to make the right decision every time. For the man who knows right from wrong and has good judgment and common sense is happier than the man who is immensely rich. You will also be given the sense to stay away from evil men and from teaching that contradicts what you know is right. Only a simpleton believes everything he's told! And an evil man is suspicious of everyone and tumbles into constant trouble. But a wise man weighs all the evidence carefully and distinguishes the true from the false.

Proverbs 2:3-5, 9, 11-15 / 3:13-15 / 8:15 / 14:15 / 17:20 / 19:27 / 20:8, 12 / 21:8 / 22:6 / 26:23-26

COMMON SENSE

Have two goals: wisdom—that is, knowing and doing right—and common sense. Don't let them slip away, for they fill you with living energy and bring you honor and respect. They keep you safe from defeat and disaster and from stumbling off the trail. Develop common sense; it is far more valuable than gold or precious jewels. Hold on tightly to all you can get. Then you will be appreciated and admired as a counselor. Yes, a wise man is known by his common sense. Those without it will be destroyed, and those who stray from it will end up dead. Wisdom is cherished in the hearts of people who have common sense, but it must shout loudly before fools will hear it.

Proverbs 2:1, 2, 7, 8 / 3:4, 5, 13-15, 21-26 / 4:5, 7 / 7:7-9 / 8:4, 5, 14 / 10:13, 21 / 11:12 / 13:15 / 14:6, 33 / 16:21 / 17:10 / 20:15 / 21:16 / 23:15, 16, 23 / 24:3, 4

KNOWLEDGE AND UNDERSTANDING

God's every word is a treasure of knowledge and understanding. The reverence and fear of God are basic to all wisdom. And wisdom is the foundation for every other kind of knowledge and understanding. So the simpleton is crowned with folly, and the wise man is crowned with knowledge. Remember, a wise man doesn't have to display his knowledge, but a fool displays his foolishness.

Proverbs 2:6 / 8:4, 5, 12 / 12:23 / 14:18 / 20:12, 24 / 30:3, 18, 19

Good Judgment

Wisdom and good judgment live together. You can't have one without the other. Learn to be wise and develop good judgment. This is very important! For such wisdom is far more valuable than precious jewels. God gives leaders good judgment so they can lead people wisely. He shows judges who is right and who is wrong. And rulers rule with his help. You may not lead a country, but you still need to use good judgment every day. For example, it would be poor judgment to become responsible for someone else's debts, or for you to favor the wicked and condemn the innocent. So develop good judgment.

Proverbs 3:13-15 / 4:5, 7 / 8:12, 14-16 / 17:18 / 18:5 / 20:8

DISCRETION

A good-looking person who lacks discretion and modesty is like a fine gold ring in a pig's snout. Watch yourself; think before you speak, or you might foolishly let some vital information slip or say something that you should not have said. A wise man holds his tongue. Only a fool blurts out everything he knows, and that only leads to sorrow and trouble. A wise man doesn't have to display his knowledge, but a fool displays his foolishness.

Proverbs 5:2 / 10:14 / 11:22 / 12:23

PRUDENCE

A prudent man is one who thinks and looks ahead! He watches for possible difficulties and problems that could come up and prepares for them. The fool attempts to fool himself by not facing facts. He never looks ahead. He goes blindly on and suffers the consequences.

Proverbs 13:16 / 14:8, 15 / 22:3 / 27:12

38

INTELLIGENCE

Get the facts, and increase your intelligence at any price. But when you are learning don't listen to teaching that contradicts the knowledge of God. It is knowing God and his knowledge that will cause you to be truly intelligent. A person who disregards God and values only worldly intelligence has missed the truth.

Proverbs 1:2-8 / 9:10 / 12:23 / 18:4 / 19:27 / 23:23 / 28:16

CAUTION

Don't be hotheaded and rush into the unknown. It's dangerous and sinful. You may start something you can't finish. From a wise mind comes careful speech and actions. Yes, a wise man is cautious and avoids danger. But a fool plunges ahead with great confidence. He ruins his chances for success by his own foolishness and then blames it on the Lord. Blessed is the man who reveres God and checks to see where he is going. The man who doesn't care is headed for serious trouble.

Proverbs 14:15, 16 / 16:23 / 19:2, 3 / 25:8-10 / 28:14

PART THREE

LEARN
AND DO

BE SENSIBLE

Wisdom is the main pursuit of sensible men, but a fool's goals are at the ends of the earth! If a man enjoys folly, something is wrong! The sensible stay on the pathways of right. Sensible sons and daughters make their parents happy, but a rebellious child makes them sad. How happy your parents will be if you turn out to be sensible! It will be a public honor to them. For when there is moral rot and foolishness within a life, a family, or even a nation, it will topple easily. With honest, sensible leaders there is stability.

Proverbs 15:20, 21 / 17:24 / 27:11, 12 / 28:2

HUMILITY

True humility and respect for the Lord lead a man to riches, honor, and long life. It is bad for men to think about all the honors they deserve. Pride goes before destruction and arrogance before a fall. Pride is sin—it disgusts the Lord, leads to arguments, and ends in destruction. A man is proud when he trusts himself! But those who use God's wisdom are safe. Yes, the Lord helps the humble.

Proverbs 3:7, 8, 34 / 6:3, 16-19 / 8:13 / 12:9 / 13:10, 16 / 14:3 / 16:5, 18, 19 / 17:19 / 18:12, 23 / 21:4, 24 / 22:4 / 25:6, 7, 27 / 26:12 / 27:2, 21 / 28:11, 26 / 29:23 / 30:32

Be Correctable

If you refuse criticism, you will end in poverty and disgrace. If you accept criticism, you are on the road to fame. Before every man there lies a wide and pleasant road that seems right, but it ends in death. It seems pleasant—that is why fools refuse to change even when they are wrong. These selfish men quarrel against what's right by demanding their own way. In their own opinion they are smarter than seven wise men. If you refuse correction you only harm yourself and your own best interests. You'll end up eating the bitter fruit of having your own way, and experiencing the full terrors of the pathway you have chosen. So don't refuse criticism; get all the help you can. You can profit from correction. When you do you'll be elected to the wise man's hall of fame. The Lord hates the stubborn. So keep an open mind. The man who is often reproved but refuses to accept criticism will suddenly be broken and never have another chance.

Proverbs 1:8, 9, 25-33 / 5:12-14 / 8:9 / 10:8, 17 / 11:20 / 12:1, 15 / 13:1, 10, 14, 18, 19 / 14:12 / 15:5, 31, 32 / 16:25 / 17:11 / 18:1 / 21:30 / 23:9, 12 / 25:11, 12 / 26:16 / 27:5, 6 / 28:14 / 29:1, 19

LISTEN TO ADVICE

The advice of a wise man refreshes like water from a mountain spring. Those accepting it become aware of the pitfalls ahead. Timely advice is as lovely as gold apples in a silver basket, and friendly suggestions are as pleasant as perfume. So listen carefully to advice and consider each suggestion. Listen and grow wise. All who do will live in peace and safety. A fool thinks he needs no advice, but a wise man listens to others. So take your parents' advice and don't despise their experience.

Proverbs 1:33 / 2:1, 2 / 4:1, 2, 10, 20-22 / 5:1 / 8:6-10, 32 / 10:8 / 11:14 / 12:15, 26 / 13:10, 14 / 14:7, 15 / 15:5, 31, 32 / 22:6 / 23:22 / 25:11, 12 / 27:5, 6, 9

45

GET ADVICE

The good man asks advice from friends; the wicked plunge ahead—and fall. Get all the advice you can and be wise the rest of your life. Don't go ahead with your plans without the advice of others. Plans go wrong with too few advisors; many advisors and wise guidance brings safety and success. Good advice lies deep within an advisor's heart. If you're wise you'll draw it out. Get all the help you can. But remember, when you're looking for advice, stay away from fools.

Proverbs 1:23 / 11:14 / 12:1, 15, 26 / 14:7 / 15:22 / 19:20 / 20:5, 18 / 23:12 / 24:6

FOLLOW INSTRUCTIONS

Follow your parents' instructions. Take to heart everything they say, and keep in mind all they tell you. Every day and all night long their words will lead you and save you from harm. When you wake up in the morning, let their instructions guide you into the next day. Yes, if you want a long and satisfying life, you must learn to follow instructions closely. Carry them out and don't forget them, for they will lead you to real living. For wise instructions are far more valuable than silver or gold and happy are all who follow them.

Proverbs 3:1, 2 / 4:13 / 6:20-23 / 7:1, 2 / 8:10, 32

DON'T FORGET

Guard the wisdom you have learned as your most precious possession. Never forget the things you've been taught. And remember the virtues you have learned. Write them deep within your heart. Don't let wisdom and common sense slip away. And never forget God's words. If you follow them, you will have a long and happy life.

Proverbs 3:1-3, 21, 24-26 / 4:4-6 / 5:7 / 6:20-23 / 7:1, 2 / 8:10, 32

GODLINESS

Godliness is a tree that bears life-giving fruit. Wickedness never brings real success; only godliness will bring that. The wicked will perish; the godly will stand. Godlessness is cruel and stubborn. It drives a man downhill, brings him trouble, and will eventually crush and destroy him. The godless live evil lives. The godly live godly lives. Godliness honors God. It is kind, reasonable, and giving. It will bring you rich rewards and real success. Godliness keeps you safe by leading you away from evil, leaving hell behind. It will lift you up and give you an exciting life full of God's favor and friendship. A curse is on those who lead the godly astray. But those who encourage godliness shall be given a worthwhile reward.

Proverbs 2:7-9, 20 / 3:21, 32 / 4:11, 12, 14, 15 / 6:16-19 / 10:2, 21 / 11:6, 11, 20, 21, 27, 30, 31 / 12:3, 6, 7, 10, 21, 28 / 13:6, 22 / 14:2, 9, 11, 14, 19, 32, 34 / 15:9, 10, 24 / 16:2, 17, 31 / 17:26 / 18:10 / 19:27 / 21:8, 12, 25, 26, 29 / 23:24, 25 / 24:1, 12, 25 / 25:26 / 28:1, 2, 10, 12, 20 / 29:7, 10

OBEDIENCE

To complain about the law is to praise wickedness. To obey the law is to fight evil. Those who are wise obey the law. But rebellious children are a grief to their fathers and a bitter blow to their mothers. If you rebel against God, the law, or your parents, you'll find yourself in trouble. And if your heart is filled with rebellion, you'll be severely punished, and the punishment will drive it out of you. The way of rebellion is heavier than sand and rocks. So don't just listen—be obedient! God blesses those who are obedient and gives them life and happiness. Obedience means life. Rebellion means death.

Proverbs 7:2, 24, 25 / 13:13 / 15:20 / 16:20 / 17:10, 11, 15, 16, 21, 25 / 18:2 / 19:16

GOODNESS

A man's goodness helps him all through life and delivers him from all kinds of trouble. Evil men are destroyed by their wickedness and their own treachery is their undoing.

Proverbs 11:6 / 13:6

LEARNING

The wise man learns by listening; the stupid person can learn only by seeing an example. He sees that example and learns when he or others are punished. A man who is taught the same thing over and over again but refuses to learn will suddenly be broken and never have another chance. When a wise man is taught, he learns and becomes wiser, and a good man will learn more and more. Yes, learning is a joy. But remember not to listen to teaching that contradicts what you know is right.

Proverbs 6:6 / 9:9 / 15:2 / 19:25, 27 / 21:11, 12 / 23:23 / 29:1, 15, 19

SUGGESTIONS

When given a suggestion, it is selfish to despise it or fight against it by insisting on doing things your own way. Friendly suggestions are as pleasant as perfume, and a wise person will consider each one.

Proverbs 15:5 / 18:1 / 27:9

ACT ON WHAT YOU KNOW

God, who knows all hearts, knows what you know and what you don't. And he rewards each person according to their deeds. In other words, he judges you by seeing how you act on what you know. So don't do something wrong or not do something right and later try to excuse yourself by saying you didn't know any better. For God knows you did, and he will hold you responsible for it.

Proverbs 24:11, 12

GROWING

As you trust in God you will flourish and grow like a tree. Just as a tree needs water, light, and pruning to grow properly, you need teaching, correction, and sometimes punishment to keep growing. So don't resent it when God or your parents discipline and correct you. Their punishment is proof of their love. They want to see you grow and have a good life. A tree starts out as a seed and takes years to grow into a fully developed tree. If a slave becomes a king or a rebel becomes prosperous, they will have trouble. God will teach you gradually, so that you can always handle what he gives you. A wise man never stops growing.

Proverbs 3:11, 12 / 9:9 / 11:28, 30 / 24:27 / 30:21-23

Searching

If you search for good you will find God's approval; if you search for evil you will find his curse. A mocker never finds the wisdom he claims he is searching for, yet it comes easily to the man with common sense. This happens because a wise man is hungry for truth, while the mocker feeds on trash. Wisdom is the main search of sensible men, but a fool's goals are at the ends of the earth! Searching for and getting wisdom is the most important thing you can do!

Proverbs 4:7 / 11:27 / 12:26 / 14:6 / 15:14 / 17:24

MEEKNESS

Wisdom hates pride and arrogance. Proud men end in shame, but the meek become wise.

Proverbs 8:13 / 11:2

GUARD WHAT YOU HEAR

A wise man is hungry for truth, while the mocker feeds on trash. Don't listen to things that contradict what you know is right. What you hear will influence everything else in your life. Guard what you hear by remembering. The upright speak what is helpful; the wicked speak rebellion. Don't listen to fools. Admire and listen to godly men, those with common sense. A curse is on anyone or anything that would lead the godly astray. But those who encourage the upright to do good shall be given a worthwhile reward.

Proverbs 4:23-27 / 10:13, 21, 31, 32 / 12:26 / 13:14 / 14:7, 15 / 15:7, 14 / 19:27

NEW IDEAS

The intelligent man is always open to new ideas. In fact, he looks for them. It is God's privilege to conceal things, and the wise man's privilege to discover and invent.

Proverbs 8:12 / 18:15 / 25:2, 3

59

THE GOOD MAN

The good man walks in the ever-brightening light of God's favor. He is covered with blessings from head to foot. A good man has firm footing, but a crook will slip and fall. The wicked man's fears will all come true, and so will the good man's hopes. The good man can look forward to happiness, while the wicked can expect only wrath. The good man finds life; the evil man finds death. Good men will be rescued from harm, but cheaters will be destroyed. The good shall never lose God's blessings, but the wicked shall lose everything. The good man's life is full of light. The sinner's road is dark and gloomy.

Proverbs 1:20-22 / 4:18, 19 / 9:9 / 10:3, 6, 7, 9, 11, 16, 20, 24, 25, 30, 31 / 11:3, 6, 8, 10, 18-20, 23, 27 / 12:2, 5, 10, 12, 17, 21, 26 / 13:2, 5, 6, 9, 25 / 14:22, 25 / 15:7, 9, 10, 19, 28 / 17:15 / 20:11 / 21:2, 4, 10, 15, 21 / 22:1 / 24 :15, 16 / 28:18, 20, 28 / 29:2, 5-7, 16, 27 / 31:10

DON'T COMPROMISE

If a godly man
compromises
with the wicked,
it is like polluting
a fountain or
muddying a spring.

Proverbs 25:26

EDUCATION

Education is a pursuit of sensible men. It is for those who have a heart for the truth. It is senseless to pay tuition to educate someone who has no desire to learn. Such a person's goals are at the ends of the earth.

Proverbs 17:16, 24

THE FACTS

Any enterprise is built by wise planning. It becomes strong through common sense and profits wonderfully by keeping abreast of the facts. The fool is only fooling himself when he doesn't care about the facts and therefore won't face them. What a shame—yes, how stupid!—to decide before knowing the facts! So get the facts, at any price.

Proverbs 14:8 / 18:1, 2, 13 / 23:22, 23 / 24: 3, 4

ADMIT YOUR MISTAKES

A man who refuses to admit his mistakes can never be successful. But if he confesses and forsakes them, he gets another chance.

Proverbs 28:13

PART FOUR

BEAUTIFUL INSIDE

MOTIVES

We can justify our every deed to other people, but God looks at our motives. God's knowledge is so amazing that he even knows the depths of hell. How much more the hearts of all mankind! A man's conscience is the Lord's searchlight exposing his hidden motives. As God looks at your motives, you should look at others. You'll learn not to associate with evil men and not to long for their favors and gifts, for their kindness is a trick. Though they pretend to be so nice, their true motives will finally come to light for all to see.

Proverbs 15:11 / 20:27 / 21:2, 3 / 23:6-8 / 26:23-26

ATTITUDE

A relaxed attitude lengthens a man's life; a bad attitude rots it away. A cheerful heart does good like medicine, but a bad attitude makes one sick. A good attitude can sustain you through any difficulty or problem, but when your attitude goes sour, your hope is gone.

Proverbs 14:30 / 15:11, 15 / 17:22 / 18:14 / 27:7

A SETTLED MIND

Everyone admires a man with a settled mind, but a man with a warped mind is despised. A settled mind comes from trusting God and knowing that he is directing your steps. With a settled mind you need not try to understand everything that happens along the way or worry about it. When you have a deep confidence in God, and his ability to work out every detail, your mind will be settled.

Proverbs 12:8 / 16:23 / 17:27, 28 / 18:14 / 20:24

A PURE HEART

Pretty words may hide a wicked heart, just as pretty glaze covers a common clay pot. A man with hate in his heart may pretend to be kind, but his hatred will finally be shown by what he does. Even the heart of a child can be known by the way he acts. God knows everyone's heart, and he will reward each person according to their deeds. So don't try to avoid responsibility for doing wrong by saying you didn't know better. For God knows your heart and he knows you did. No one can ever say, "I have cleansed my heart; I am sinless." Silver and gold are purified by fire, but only God can purify your heart. Trust him.

Proverbs 17:3 / 20:9, 11, 30 / 24:11, 12 / 26:23-26

FILLING YOUR HEART

Deceit fills hearts that are planning evil; joy fills hearts that are planning good. If a youngster's heart is filled with rebellion, punishment will drive it out of him. The wise fill their hearts with wisdom. They are hungry for truth, while the mocker fills his heart with trash. If you fill your heart with negative thoughts, they will destroy your hope. And hope that is frustrated makes the heart sick. But if you fill your heart with the positive thoughts of God's Word, your dreams will come true at last. Then you'll have life and joy.

Proverbs 12:20, 25 / 13:12 / 14:13, 33 / 15:11, 14 / 17:22 / 20:5 / 22:15 / 23:29, 30

YOUR SOUL

I
f you value your soul, you will stay off the thorny, treacherous road of the rebel. You will also keep away from angry, short-tempered men, for in their company you might learn to be like them and again endanger your soul. And if you value your soul you won't sell it for a piece of bread either. And that's exactly what you're doing when you give preferred treatment to rich people.

Proverbs 22:5, 24 / 28:21

AN OPEN MIND

God's wisdom is plain and clear to anyone with half a mind—if it is only open! An evil man has a closed mind, but a godly man will reconsider. Yes, an intelligent mind is always open to new ideas. In fact, it looks for them.

Proverbs 8:9 / 18:15 / 21:29

72

SIN

If anyone respects and fears God, he will hate evil. For wisdom hates pride, arrogance, corruption, and deceit of every kind. Ignoring sin leads to sorrow; speaking out against sin leads to peace. To do right honors God. Blessings chase the righteous! To sin is to despise God. Sin brings disgrace, and the wicked are crushed beneath their load of sins. Curses chase sinners. Who can say, "I have cleansed my heart; I am sinless"? Sin is atoned for by mercy and truth; evil is avoided by respect for God.

Proverbs 8:13 / 10:10, 16 / 11:5 / 13:21, 22 / 14:2, 32, 34 / 16:6 / 17:19 / 18:3 / 19:28 / 20:9

RIGHTEOUSNESS

The Lord is far from the wicked, but he hears the prayers of the righteous. The Lord preserves and protects the righteous. Yes, the man who wants to do right will get a rich reward. Curses chase sinners, while blessings chase the righteous! Your riches won't help you on Judgment Day; only righteousness counts then. God ruins the plans of the wicked and they are destroyed. The man who tries to be good, loving, and kind finds life, righteousness, and honor. Righteousness is a reward of wisdom. The wicked will finally lose; the righteous will finally win.

Proverbs 8:18, 20 / 10:16, 29 / 11:4, 5 / 13:21 / 15:21, 29 / 20:11 / 21: 18, 21 / 22:12 / 28:20

CONSCIENCE

A man's conscience is the Lord's searchlight exposing his hidden motives. When you have done something wrong, your conscience should cut at you like a two-edged sword. It's letting you know wrong from right. Those who ignore their conscience and keep on sinning must really hate themselves. They know the consequences of sinning but do it anyway. When a man stops listening to his conscience by arguing, "What's wrong with that?" his conscience will be silenced like a murderer's. And a silenced conscience will drive him into hell! But if you listen to your conscience you'll stay away from sin and on the path to life.

Proverbs 5:3, 4 / 20:27 / 28:17, 24 / 29:24 / 30:11, 12, 20

75

HATE EVIL

If anyone respects and fears God, he will hate evil. For wisdom hates pride, arrogance, corruption, and deceit of every kind. The Lord despises those who say that bad is good and good is bad. To complain about the law is to praise wickedness. To obey the law is to fight evil. Don't even enjoy the company of evil men, or you will become like them. The wicked enjoy fellowship with others who are wicked; liars enjoy being around other liars. The good hate the badness of the wicked. The wicked hate the goodness of the good.

Proverbs 8:13 / 13:5, 20 / 15:27 / 17:4, 15 / 20:30 / 24:1, 2 / 28:4, 12, 16/ 29:27

TEMPTATION

I f people involved in doing the wrong things tell you, "Come and join us," turn your back on them. Run from sin! Don't go near it, for you might fall into temptation. Don't let your desires get out of hand! The fruit of sin may look sweet, but sinners are doomed by their own sins. The sins become ropes that catch and hold them. Watch your step. Stick to the right path and be safe. Pull back your foot from temptation. Can a man hold fire against his chest and not be burned? Can he walk on hot coals and not blister his feet? When you play with temptation you are like an ox going to the butcher, or a deer that is trapped, waiting to be killed with an arrow through his heart. You are like a bird flying into a snare, not knowing the fate awaiting it there.

Proverbs 1:10-19 / 4:24-27 / 5:1-23 / 6:24-28 / 7:1-27 / 9:17, 18

AFFECTIONS

A bove all else, guard your affections. For they influence everything else in your life.

Proverbs 4:23 / 7:25 / 8:13 / 24:1, 2

THOUGHTS

A good man's mind is filled with honest thoughts; an evil man's mind is crammed with lies. The Lord hates the thoughts of the wicked. An evil man uses his thoughts to plan evil deeds and to think up new schemes that stir up trouble everywhere. This man will be destroyed. Don't let yourself think evil thoughts! Let God's Word and your parents' advice be beams of light directed into the dark corners of your mind. They warn you of danger and give you a good life.

Proverbs 4:21, 22 / 6:14, 15, 23 / 7:1-3, 25 / 12:5 / 15:11, 26, 28 / 16:23, 30

FACES

A happy face means a glad heart, and that does good like medicine. A sad face means a breaking heart, and that can make one sick. So cheer up and smile.

Proverbs 15:13, 15 / 17:22

PART FIVE

DEPEND-ABILITY

FAITHFULNESS

Trusting an unfaithful person is as foolish as cutting off your feet and drinking poison! But trusting a faithful person is as refreshing as a cool day in the hot summertime.

Proverbs 12:22 / 13:17 / 18:24 / 25:13, 19 / 26:6 / 27:8

RELIABILITY

A reliable man is honest and sensible. He will bring stability to anything he does. People can depend on a reliable man. But putting confidence in an unreliable man is like chewing with a sore tooth, or trying to win a race on a broken foot.

Proverbs 3:17 / 12:22 / 18:24 / 25:19 / 26:6 / 28:2

LOYALTY

A true friend is always loyal, and a brother is born to help in time of need. Most people will tell you what loyal friends they are, but are they telling the truth? There are "friends" who pretend to be friends, but there is a friend who sticks closer than a brother. Never abandon a friend—either yours or your father's. Then you won't need to go to a distant relative for help in your time of need.

Proverbs 17:17 / 18:19, 24 / 19:7 / 20:6 / 27:10

BEING TRUSTWORTHY

A trustworthy man can be trusted with your most prized possessions and your closest secrets. An untrustworthy man doesn't care about your interests, and he'll even spread rumors. The trustworthy man will try to quiet them.

Proverbs 11:13 / 27:18

KEEPING PROMISES

God delights in those who keep their promises and
hates those who don't. A person who doesn't give
the gift he promised is like a cloud blowing over
a desert without dropping any rain. So count the cost of
your promise before making it to the Lord or anyone else;
it's foolish not to.

Proverbs 12:22 / 20:25 / 25:14

RESPONSIBILITY

God will reward everyone according to his deeds, so you are responsible for everything you do. You are held responsible for obeying God's Word and helping others. And after you've done something wrong or not done what you were supposed to do, don't try to avoid responsibility by saying you didn't know any better. For God knows that you did. It is poor judgment to take on someone else's responsibilities, like countersigning for another's debt. If you work for someone, you are looking after their interests and responsibilities. For this you should be rewarded.

Proverbs 17:17, 18 / 19:3 / 24:11, 12 / 27:18

HONESTY

A little gained honestly is better than great wealth gotten by dishonest means. It is better to be poor and honest than rich and dishonest. Some men enjoy cheating, but the cake they buy with such ill-gotten gain will turn to gravel in their mouths. Dishonest gain will never last, so why take the risk? The Lord loathes all cheating and dishonesty. A good man is guided by his honesty and has a firm footing; the crook is destroyed by his dishonesty. Honesty is its own defense.

Proverbs 10:9 / 11:1, 3, 5 / 12:5, 13 / 16:8 / 17:26 / 19:1, 22 / 20:7, 10, 17, 23, 28 / 21:6, 28 / 28:2, 6, 16

TRUTH

Many things you hear may sound true, but when you compare them with God's Word the record is set straight. For God's Word is living truth. It will stand the test of time. But falsehoods are soon exposed. A rebel cares nothing for truth. Therefore he lets himself be led away into incredible folly and deception, which endanger his life. So learn God's Word. As you do, truth will enter the very center of your being, filling your life with joy. He who values grace and truth is God's friend.

Proverbs 2:10 / 5:23 / 8:6, 7 / 10:11 / 12:19 / 16:6 / 17:16 / 18:17 / 19:28 / 22:11 / 30:5

TRUSTING OTHERS

Only a simpleton believes everything he's told! A sensible man understands the need for proof. But an evil man goes too far—he is suspicious of everyone and tumbles into constant trouble. So don't be suspicious, but be cautious. Trust others to do what you know they can do. But don't give anyone responsibilities beyond what he can handle. Don't count on someone who breaks his promises. Don't trust a rebel to convey a message. Don't put confidence in an unreliable man. And don't believe the kindness of a man with hate in his heart. To believe that your success or failure depends on others is called the fear of man. That is a dangerous trap. To trust in God means safety.

Proverbs 12:22 / 13:17 / 14:15 / 17:20 / 18:24 / 20:6 / 23:1-3 / 25:19 / 26:6, 24-26 / 29:25 / 31:11

PART SIX

SPEAKING THE TRUTH

FRANKNESS

In the end, people appreciate frankness more than flattery. Open criticism from a caring person is better than hidden love! Wounds from a friend are better than kisses from an enemy! Yes, it is an honor to receive a frank reply.

Proverbs 24:26 / 26:18, 19 / 27:5, 6 / 28:23

TELLING THE TRUTH

The Lord hates lying and every kind of deception. Everything he says is right and true. A good man also hates lies. His mind is filled with honest thoughts, and there is living truth and great satisfaction in everything he says. His words help others because they can trust what he says. Lying, and then saying, "I was just fooling," or trying to get even with someone by lying about them is as harmful as hitting someone with an axe. Worthless and wicked men are constant liars. Their minds are crammed with lies, and what they say is shunned. Liars will be punished and come to shame. Lying will get anyone into trouble, but an honest person is safe because honesty is its own defense. Truth stands the test of time, but lies are soon exposed.

Proverbs 3:3 / 6:12, 13, 16-19 / 8:6, 7, 13 / 10:11, 31 / 12:5, 13, 14, 17, 19 / 13:5 / 14:5, 25 / 17:4, 7 / 18:17 / 19:5 / 20:6, 17, 21 / 21:28 / 24:28, 29 / 25:18 / 26:18, 19 / 30:6

TALKING ABOUT OTHERS

A gossip goes around spreading rumors, while a trustworthy man tries to quiet them. An evil man sows arguments; gossip separates the best of friends. Idle lips are the devil's mouthpiece. To slander is to be a fool. So don't say negative things about your friends and neighbors, not even to pay them back for being mean to you. Go and discuss the matter with them privately. Don't tell anyone else. Fire goes out for lack of fuel, and tensions disappear when gossip stops. You should use your words to defend others and to speak up for those who can't help themselves. God delights in kind words, and good reports bring happiness and health. Let kindness be the rule for everything you say.

Proverbs 10:14, 18 / 11:9, 13 / 12:18 / 15:26, 30 / 16:27, 28 / 17:5, 9 / 18:8, 21 / 20:19 / 24:28, 29 / 15:8-10, 18 / 26:20, 22, 23 / 30:10, 11, 32 / 31:8, 9, 26

OVERLOOKING INSULTS

A fool is quick-tempered; a wise man stays cool when insulted. Don't repay evil for evil. Wait for the Lord to handle the matter. Self-control means controlling the tongue! A quick retort can ruin everything. A gentle answer turns away anger, but harsh words cause quarrels. To quarrel with a neighbor is foolish; a man with good sense holds his tongue. A wise man restrains his anger and overlooks insults. This is to his credit.

Proverbs 10:11, 12 / 11:12 / 12:16 / 13:2, 3 / 15:1 / 17:9, 14 / 18:2, 6, 21 / 19:11 / 20:22 / 21:23 / 25:15, 23 / 26:4, 5 / 29:8, 9, 19 / 30:32

WHOLESOME TALK

There is living truth in what a good man says, but the mouth of the evil man is filled with curses. When a good man speaks, he is worth listening to, but the words of fools are a dime a dozen. A rebel's foolish talk should prick his own pride! But the wise man's speech is respected. A good man thinks before he speaks; the evil man pours out his evil words without a thought. Remember, men have died for saying the wrong thing!

Proverbs 10:11, 12, 20 / 11:9 / 12:23 / 14:3 / 15:1, 2, 28 / 16:27 / 18:4, 21 / 20:20 / 21:24 / 26:2 / 29:8, 9 / 30:10, 32 / 31:26

CONVERSATION

A friendly conversation is as stimulating as the sparks that fly when iron strikes iron. If you want a good and friendly conversation, remember these guidelines.

- Listen! A man of few words and a settled mind is wise.
- Don't argue!
- It is hard to stop a quarrel once it starts, so don't let it begin.
- Don't nag!
- Love forgets mistakes; nagging about them parts the best of friends.
- Be kind!
- Let kindness be the rule for everything you say.
- Don't gossip!
- A gossip goes around spreading rumors, while a trust-worthy man tries to quiet them.
- Be calm and gentle!
- Harsh words cause quarrels.
- Be positive!
- Good reports give happiness and health.

Proverbs 10:20 / 11:12, 13 / 12:25 / 15:1, 30 / 16:27, 28 / 17:9, 14, 27, 28 / 26:4, 5 / 27:17 / 31:26

POWER OF WORDS

Evil words destroy. Idle lips are the devil's mouthpiece. The wrong words can bring discouragement and even separate the best of friends. Your mouth can be your undoing. Your words can put you and others in danger. Men have died for saying the wrong thing. Saying the wrong thing to someone or about someone, even when you're just joking, can be as harmful as hitting them with an axe or wounding them with a sword. But the words of the wise are helpful; they soothe and heal. And a word of encouragement can do wonders. Yes, good and kind words are enjoyable. They cause life, happiness, and health. A soft tongue can break through any barrier. So think before you speak, because you can't withdraw what you've said.

Proverbs 10:14, 32 / 11:9 / 12:18, 25 / 13:3 / 15:1, 4, 30 / 16:24, 27, 28 / 17:9 / 18:6, 7, 21 / 25:10, 15, 18, 23 / 26:2, 18, 19 / 27:17 / 30:32 / 31:26

TALKING

T hink before you speak. How wonderful it is to be able to say the right thing at the right time! When you talk, what you say should be worth listening to, thoughtful, and wise. What you say should be respected. If you're in a discussion, win your case by careful argument. There should be living truth in everything you say.

Proverbs 10:11, 20 / 12:18, 25 / 13:2, 3 / 14:3, 23 / 15:4, 23, 26, 28 / 16:24 / 17:9 / 18:2, 6, 7, 23 / 23:15, 16

HUMBLE SPEECH

There is one thing worse than a fool, and that is a man who is conceited. He praises himself and even brags about his own foolishness. Boasting is looking for trouble. It leads to arguments and destruction. So don't praise yourself; let others do it! And if you're about to brag—cover your mouth with your hand in shame. Be humble, listen to others, and become wise.

Proverbs 3:7, 8, 34 / 13:10, 16 / 14:3 / 16:18 / 17:19 / 18:23 / 21:24 / 26:12 / 27:2 / 30:32

COMMUNICATION

n unreliable messenger can cause a lot of trouble.
Reliable communication permits progress.
Proverbs 13:17

PERSUASIVE SPEECH

If you want something from others, like cooperation, help, or anything else, you must be persuasive. You can't beg and plead like a desperate man, and you can't demand things like a rich man might. And don't try to persuade others by griping and complaining about your problems and needs. Win your case with careful and persuasive speech, then others will consider it a joy to help you.

Proverbs 13:2 / 15:2, 4 / 16:23 / 18:23

102

FLATTERY

Flattery is a form of hatred and wounds cruelly. Flattery is a trap; evil men are caught in it, but good men stay away and sing for joy. The wicked use compliments and flattery to pull you into their wickedness. Though what they say seems as sweet as honey, don't listen, because it's a lie. Flattery is their stock-in-trade. It will lead you to death and hell. Only wisdom from the Lord can save you from it. And don't flatter others. In the end, people appreciate frankness more than flattery.

Proverbs 2:16, 17 / 5:3-5 / 6:24 / 7:4, 5 / 26:28 / 28:23 / 29:5, 6

TALK LITTLE

Don't talk so much. You keep putting your foot in your mouth. Be sensible and turn off the flow! When a good man speaks, he is worth listening to, but the words of fools are a dime a dozen. A wise man doesn't display his knowledge. Only a fool blurts out everything he knows, and that only leads to sorrow and trouble. The man of few words and settled mind is wise; therefore, even a fool is thought to be wise when he is silent. It pays him to keep his mouth shut. Keep your mouth closed and you'll stay out of trouble.

Proverbs 10:14, 19, 20 / 11:12 / 12:23 / 14:23 / 15:23, 28 / 17:27, 28 / 18:4, 21 / 20:19 / 21:23 / 23:15, 16 / 30:32

PART SEVEN

HOME AND FAMILY

MARRIAGE

A father can give his children homes and riches, but only the Lord can give them understanding mates. Yes, that is a blessing from the Lord. So trust God to bring you the right mate at the right time. A good mate is a joy, but the other kind corrodes your strength and tears down everything you do. A good mate is worth more than precious gems! You can trust her and she will richly satisfy your needs. She will not hinder you but will help you all your life. Charm can be deceptive and beauty doesn't last, but a mate who fears and reverences God shall be greatly praised.

Proverbs 5:15, 18, 19 / 12:4 / 18:22 / 19:13, 14 / 21:9, 19 / 25:24 / 27:4 / 30:18, 19, 21-23 / 31:10-12, 30

FINDING A MATE

The Book of Proverbs lists four things that are too wonderful to understand. One of them is "the growth of love between a man and a woman." But listen to wisdom! If you have dedicated yourself and your life to the Lord, than he has a perfect time for that to happen. So don't spend all your time dating and looking for sweethearts. God has other parts of your life he wants to order first. An understanding husband or wife is from the Lord. So if you wait for God's match, your marriage will be worth more than precious gems!

Proverbs 7:4 / 24:27 / 30:18, 19 / 31:2, 3, 10-12, 30

LISTEN TO YOUR PARENTS

Obey your father and mother. Take to heart all of their advice; keep in mind everything they tell you. Every day and all night long their counsel will lead you and save you from harm. When you wake up in the morning, let their instructions guide you into the new day. What you learn from them will stand you in good stead; it will gain you many honors. Only a fool despises his parents' advice. Listen to your father's advice and don't despise your mother's experience. The father of godly children has cause for joy—what pleasure a wise son or daughter is! So give your parents joy.

Proverbs 1:8, 9 / 6:20-24 / 13:1-24 / 15:5, 20 / 17:1 / 20:29 / 23:22-25 / 30:11, 12, 17

A WISE SON
OR DAUGHTER

Wise children are godly. Children with common sense use thoughtful, wise words. They obey the law and are levelheaded and sensible. Wise children listen to their parents. The parents of these children are happy, and they rejoice at how their sons and daughters act. Their hearts thrill and have cause for joy. Their children are a public honor to them and have given them peace of mind. A rebellious child is a calamity to his parents. And children who mistreat their father or mother are a public disgrace.

Proverbs 3:11, 12 / 10:1 / 13:24 / 15:5, 20 / 17:2, 21, 25 / 19:13, 26 / 23:15, 16, 24, 25 / 27:11 / 28:7, 24 / 29:3, 15, 17

FAMILY

Accept wisdom as a beloved member of your family. For wickedness brings grief to a family, but wisdom brings happiness. Love your family and be kind to them. The fool who provokes his family to anger and resentment will finally have nothing worthwhile left; he shall be the servant of a wiser man.

Proverbs 7:4 / 8:31 / 11:21, 29 / 15:27

CHILDREN

Children with godly parents have a place of refuge and security. Yes, you can be very sure God will rescue the children of the godly. But children can't just rely on their parents' godliness. Even children can be known by the way they act—whether what they do is pure and right. And they are held responsible for their own actions. So if parents don't discipline their children, it proves they don't love them. For if they love their children, they will be prompt to punish them. Punishment will drive rebellion out of them, keeping them from hell and giving them a good life. Yes, if children are taught to choose the right path, when they are older they will remain on it.

Proverbs 6:20-23 / 11:21 / 13:24 / 14:26 / 20:11 / 22:6, 15 / 23:13, 14, 24, 25 / 27:11 / 29:15-17 / 31:2, 3, 28, 29

PARENTS

Your parents should be your glory and pride. Respect them, love them, bless them, thank them, talk well of them, and treat them well. It is a wonderful heritage to have godly parents. Children who mistreat their parents are a public disgrace. God puts out the light of a man who curses his father or mother. And a person who mocks his father and despises his mother shall have his eye plucked out by ravens and eaten by vultures.

Proverbs 17:6 / 19:14, 26 / 20:7, 20 / 30:11, 12, 17

DISCIPLINE

Sometimes mere words are not enough—discipline is needed. This happens when you are not obeying what your parents are saying. You need to be disciplined when you are young while there is still lots of hope for you. If your parents don't discipline you, they will ruin your life. Your parents' discipline won't really hurt you. And you won't die if they spank you. But their punishment will keep you out of hell by teaching you that wrong actions end in suffering. Yes, scoldings and spankings help you learn.

Proverbs 13:24 / 19:18 / 23:13, 14 / 29:15, 17-19

GRANDPARENTS

It is good to respect your parents, for they are your glory and pride. But also respect your grandparents. They helped your parents to be who they are today. And you, being the proof that your grandparents did a great job of raising your mother or father, are their glory and pride. Gray hair and wrinkles are signs of experience, and with that experience comes wisdom. Yes, godliness and wisdom are a priceless inheritance passed down to you from godly grandparents.

Proverbs 13:22 / 16:31 / 17:6

YOUR HOME

It is better to live in the corner of an attic than in a beautiful home with cranky, quarrelsome, and complaining people. It is better to have a little with reverence for God than to have great treasure and trouble with it. A dry crust eaten in a peaceful home is better than steak every day in a home full of argument and strife. So don't be miserable when you are at home. That's when it is the most important to be nice, cheerful, and easy to get along with.

Proverbs 15:16, 17 / 17:1, 13 / 18:10 / 19:23 / 21:9, 19 / 24:27 / 25:24 / 27:8

BROTHERS AND SISTERS

Abrother or sister is born to help in time of need. God's intended purpose for brothers and sisters is for them to help each other. Don't be embarrassed by your brothers and sisters, and don't ignore them when they call on you for help. Be their best friends. For it is harder to win back the friendship of an offended brother than to capture a fortified city. And you'll need their help one day, too.

Proverbs 17:17 / 18:19, 24 / 19:7 / 27:10

116

PART EIGHT

FRIENDS AND NEIGHBORS

COMMUNITY

The Book of Proverbs lists four things that are small but unusually wise. One of them is the locusts, because though they have no leader, they stay together in swarms. Like the locusts, people also stay together in groups. These groups are called communities. Your community consists of your family, your friends, and your neighbors. Since people enjoy fellowship with others like themselves, you'll usually find the wicked with the wicked and the godly with the godly. If you're in a community of mostly godly people, rejoice, because the good influence of godly citizens causes a community to prosper. But the moral decay of the wicked drives it downhill.

Proverbs 11:10-13 / 17:4 / 28:28 / 30:24-28

FELLOWSHIP

A mirror reflects a man's face, but what he is really like is shown by the kind of friends he chooses. People enjoy fellowship with others who are like themselves. So don't fellowship with the wicked and don't enjoy their company. For wickedness loves company—and leads others into sin. Avoid even the places where the wicked spend their time. Go somewhere else. Be with wise men and become wise. If you stay with evil men you will become evil. Even God stays far from the wicked and gives his friendship to the godly. Keep away from rebels and angry, short-tempered men, for you might learn to be like them and endanger your soul. And don't fellowship with drunkards, gluttons, and lazy people, or you'll follow them to poverty. And don't think that you won't be affected if you just spend a little time fellowshipping with the wicked. It only takes a small amount of pollution to make all of the water in a fountain or spring dirty.

Proverbs 1:10-19 / 2:11-15 / 3:30-32 / 4:14-19 / 13:20 / 14:1, 2, 21, 22 / 16:7, 29 / 17:4 / 21:8 / 22:24, 25 / 23:19-21 / 25:26 / 27:19 / 28:7 / 29:24, 27

KINDNESS

Never get tired of being kind. Hold on to this virtue tightly and let it always be the motivation of your heart. Kindness makes you attractive, so let kindness be the rule for everything you say and do. And remember, your own soul is nourished when you are kind; it is destroyed when you are cruel.

Proverbs 3:3 / 11:16, 17 / 12:10 / 15:26 / 16:24 / 19:22 / 20:28 / 21:21 / 23:6-8 / 26:24-26 / 31:26

SELF-CONTROL

Self-control means controlling your tongue, your temper, and anything else that needs controlling, like your appetite and your desires. It is better to have self-control than to control an army. And a person without it is as defenseless or as open to destruction as a city at war with no protection.

Proverbs 13:3, 25 / 16:32 / 25:28

AN EVEN TEMPER

Being even-tempered is better than being famous. Stay away from short-tempered people. If you don't, you'll end up just like them. When you are angry you make mistakes, start fights, and get into all kinds of trouble that endangers your soul. Fools and rebels have quick tempers. A wise man stays cool and is patient. By controlling your temper and refusing to shout and argue, you prevent fights, stay out of trouble and keep your friends. There is more hope for a fool than for people with quick tempers.

Proverbs 12:16 / 14:17, 29 / 15:18 / 16:32 / 19:11, 19 / 22:24 / 29:9, 11, 20, 22 / 30:33

LOVE

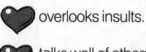

overlooks insults.

talks well of others.

forgets mistakes.

does not nag.

does not quarrel.

uses kind words.

is honest.

rebukes and corrects.

is forgiving.

listens and cares.

delights in the success of others.

is helpful.

is not just a feeling. It's unselfish and
giving, and it is proved by unselfish actions.
If you refuse to do these things,
you are not acting in love.
But those who search for and desire
to move in love, will know God.

Proverbs 3:11 / 8:17 / 10:12, 18 / 13:24 / 17:9 / 18:21 / 27:5 / 29:10

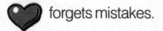

123

CARING FOR OTHERS

The wicked are jealous of other people's successes. They rejoice at other's misfortunes. The good care for others and long to help them. God wants us to care about people just like he does. When we care for others we become willing to help them. Care for people who can't help themselves. If you see someone hungry or thirsty, give them food and something to drink. If someone is discouraged, encourage them with gentle words. If someone needs your help, give them a hand. Defend those who can't defend themselves. And be sensitive to someone whose heart is heavy. Income gotten from taking advantage of other's misfortunes will end up in the hands of someone who will care for them. In every way you care for others, God will care for you.

Proverbs 12:12 / 14:21 / 15:4, 25 / 17:5 / 21:13 / 25:20-22 / 28:8 / 29:7 / 31:8, 9

GENEROSITY

The selfish man is only concerned for himself. He is greedy and demands his own way. The generous man thinks of others and loves to give. Don't beg favors from a generous man, and don't become his friend just to get something. If you do, you are greedy. Instead, learn from him and go find those who need your favors and gifts.

Generosity is the key to prosperity!

Proverbs 18:1 / 19:6 / 21:25, 26/ 22:9

NEIGHBORS

Be a good neighbor. Be friendly and always willing to help. Neighbors should trust each other and look after each other's interests. Don't betray that trust with your words, by speaking against them, or with your actions, by plotting evil against them. To quarrel with a neighbor is foolish. And remember, your neighbors are all those people who live around you, not just the people you happen to like. Always be friendly with your neighbors, but don't visit them too often, or you will outwear your welcome.

Proverbs 3:29 / 11:12 / 14:20, 21 / 21:10 / 24:28, 29 / 25:8-10, 17 / 26:18, 19

TREAT ALL PEOPLE THE SAME

God gives light to both the rich and the poor. To treat some people differently than others because of how they look, what talents they have, how much money they have, or even because they treat you wrongly is not good. You are being sinful if you look down on someone because they're poor or because you think there is something wrong with them. And giving preferred treatment to rich people is a clear case of selling one's soul for a piece of bread. Be kind, just, and fair with everyone and you will be blessed.

Proverbs 14:20, 21 / 17:23 / 24:23 / 25:4, 5, 21, 22 / 28:12, 21 / 29:13, 14

GETTING ALONG

Wise men try to keep peace. It is an honor for a man to always get along with others. To get along with everyone and avoid fights follow these simple rules:

- Don't even think of being violent.
- Don't allow hatred to enter your heart.
- Overlook insults.
- Don't argue.
- Hold your tongue.
- Be humble and take advice.
- Always answer harsh words gently.
- Be cool-tempered.
- Don't gossip.
- Forget mistakes.
- Don't nag.
- Don't yell.
- Don't insist on your own way.
- Love peace.

Proverbs 1:19 / 3:30-32 / 10:12 / 11:12 / 13:2, 10 / 15:1, 18 / 16:28 / 17:1, 9, 13, 14, 19 / 18:2, 6, 7, 18, 19 / 20:3 / 21:14, 29 / 22:10 / 25:21, 22, 26 / 26:20, 21 / 27:17 / 28:25 / 29:8, 10, 11, 22 / 30:33

HELPING OTHERS

The common bond of sinful people is their guilt. They feel guilty because they are selfish and can't bring themselves to help others. The common bond of godly people is good will. They long to help each other. Even the words they speak are helpful. Never refuse to help a brother or a sister or a friend. Then you won't need to go to a distant relative for help in your time of need. And remember, if you keep shutting your ears to requests for help, you will also be ignored in your time of need.

Proverbs 10:32 / 11:24-26 / 12:12, 25 / 14:9 / 15:25 / 17:5, 17 / 19:17, 19 / 21:13 / 24:11, 12 / 25:21, 22 / 27:10, 18 / 28:8, 21, 27 / 31:8, 9, 12, 19, 20

FRIENDS

A true friend is always loyal. Most people will tell you what loyal friends they are, but are they telling the truth? There are "friends" who pretend to be friends, but a real friend will stick closer than a brother. If you turn away from a friend when he needs you, you are not a true friend. If you were, you would never abandon him.

Proverbs 12:26 / 13:20 / 14:7, 9, 20, 21 / 15:17 / 16:7, 28, 29 / 17:4, 9, 17 / 18:19, 24 / 19:4, 6, 7 / 20:6 / 25:17 / 27:4, 6, 9, 10, 14, 17, 19

WINNING SOULS

As you live a godly life, you are growing a tree that bears life-giving fruit. It is life-giving because those who observe your life will see the results of knowing God, and come to know him themselves. But let God prepare the hearts of those around you. It is senseless to share your faith in God with someone who has no heart for truth. And if you offend them it will be harder to win them later. All who win souls are wise.

Proverbs 11:3 / 17:16 / 18:19

BE PLEASANT

If you are pleasant, people will consider you a good person to be with. But in order to be pleasant all of the time you need to consider how other people feel. For example, if you shout a pleasant greeting to a friend too early in the morning, he will not be too happy about it. And being happy-go-lucky around a person who is extremely sad is as bad as stealing his jacket in cold weather, or rubbing salt in his wounds.

Proverbs 3:3 / 11:17 / 16:21 / 17:22 / 19:22 / 21:21 / 25:20-22, 24 / 26:24-26 / 27:14, 15

132

RESPECT OTHERS' BELONGINGS

Young toughs have no respect for the belongings of others. They steal what they want and vandalize what they can't have. They also enjoy cheating people out of what is rightfully theirs. Crime is their way of life. They don't realize that those who act this way become citizens of hell. Stay away from people like that. And treat the belongings of others as you would have them treat what is yours.

Proverbs 1:10-18 / 6:30, 31 / 9:17, 18 / 10:2 / 20:17 / 22:7, 22, 23 / 23:10, 11 / 26:27

ENCOURAGEMENT

If you are encouraged, you can make it through any difficulty, but when discouragement sets in, what hope is left? A curse on those who discourage the godly and cause them to fall off the path. But men who encourage the upright to do good and keep on going will be given a worthwhile reward. If you know someone with a heavy heart, don't let him stew in his sadness, for that will discourage him further. Give him a word of encouragement. That will do wonders.

Proverbs 12:2, 6, 25 / 15:4 / 17:5 / 18:14 / 28:10

GENTLENESS

Gentleness
and
gentle
words
will
turn
away
wrath
and
give
life
and
health
to
yourself
and
those
to
whom
you
speak
gently.

*Proverbs
15:1, 4*

AGREEMENT

When all the people you must consult and all the people that are involved agree, then go ahead with your plans. If you all can't agree, then stop, take the advice of others, and change your plans.

Proverbs 20:18

PEER PRESSURE

Being afraid of what other people think of you is a dangerous trap. So if sinners want you to join them, just turn your back. Don't let them pressure you into doing as they do. To avoid their pressure, just don't go where they spend their time. The constant influence of these ungodly people will drive you downhill. Go somewhere else and let the good influence of godly people cause you to become wise and prosperous. Be like a bird, who stays away when it sees a trap being set. Trust God for good friends and you'll be given the sense to stay away from evil.

Proverbs 1:10-19 / 2:11-15 / 4:14, 15 / 11:11 / 13:20 / 17:4 / 22:24, 25 / 24:1, 2 / 25:26 / 27:19 / 28:28 / 29:18, 24, 25

MIND YOUR OWN BUSINESS

Yanking a dog's ears is no more foolish than inter-fering with something that isn't any of your busi-ness.

Proverbs 26:17

UNITY

The Lord hates evil men who cause arguments and fights in families, in churches, or among neighbors. These men are selfish. They speak rebellion and tell lies in order to lead others out of unity and into rebellion with them. Don't listen to them and don't say or do anything that would cause disunity and strife. For nothing a family or any other group of people does will succeed without unity.

Proverbs 6:16-19 / 10:32 / 15:28, 29 / 20:18 / 30:24-28

SOW AND REAP

The man who sets a trap for others will get caught in it himself. Roll a boulder down on someone, and it will roll back and crush you. Because the wicked are unfair, their violence boomerangs and destroys them. But the generous man shall be rich! By watering others, he waters himself.

Proverbs 11:24, 25 / 21:7 / 22:8 / 26:27

VISITING

Don't visit your neighbor too often, or you will wear out your welcome!
Proverbs 25:17

FORGIVENESS

He who values forgiveness and truth is the king's friend. So do not rejoice when your enemy meets trouble. Let there be no gladness when he falls, for the Lord may be displeased with you. If your enemy is hungry, give him food! If he is thirsty, give him something to drink! This will make him feel ashamed of himself, and God will reward you.

Proverbs 22:11 / 24:15-18 / 25:21, 22

PART NINE

REPUTATION

HONOR

he wise are promoted to honor, but fools end up in shame! And those who fall into temptation will lose their honor. Yes, honor doesn't go with fools any more than snow with summertime or a hot day in winter! Giving honor to a mean person will backfire like a stone tied to a slingshot. True humility and respect for the Lord will lead you to honor. And the man who tries to be good, loving, and kind will find it.

Proverbs 1:8, 9 / 3:9, 10, 16, 17, 35 / 4:8, 9 / 5:7-9 / 8:17, 18 / 11:16 / 14:2, 31 / 15:33 / 18:12 / 20:3 / 21:21 / 22:4 / 25:27 / 26:1, 8 / 27:11 / 29:23

FAVOR

If you want favor with both God and man, then trust the
Lord completely; don't ever trust yourself alone.
Then you will walk along in the ever-brightening
light of God's favor. And the dawn will give
way to morning splendor.

*Proverbs 3:4-6 / 4:18, 19 / 11:27 /
16:15 / 18:5 / 19:6 / 23:6-8*

REPUTATION
(A GOOD NAME)

If you must choose, take a good name rather than great riches; for to be held in loving esteem is better than silver and gold. We all have happy memories of good men gone to their reward, but the names of wicked men stink after them.

Proverbs 3:4-6, 21, 22 / 10:7, 13 / 12:17 / 13:5 / 14:3, 24 / 18:3 / 22:1

POPULARITY

When you are trying to please God, God will make even your worst enemies to be at peace with you. And if even your enemies are at peace with you, you will be a very popular person in your community. Yes, if you value grace and truth you will even be friends with leaders, public figures, and royalty. But as your success and popularity grow, learn to recognize who your real friends are. For a wealthy and popular man has many people calling themselves his "friends."

Proverbs 3:4, 5 / 11:10 / 13:18 / 14:20, 21 / 16:7 / 18:6, 7 / 19:4 / 20:6 / 22:11

BEING PRAISED AND APPRECIATED

A man with good sense is appreciated. And wise men are praised for their wisdom. When others praise you and let you know that you are appreciated, remember, a man is tested by his reaction to praise. Thank them and be encouraged, but don't let it go to your head. Also, learn to recognize flattery, for flattery is a dangerous trap.

Proverbs 12:25 / 13:15 / 14:24 / 23:6-8 / 26:28 / 27:2, 21 / 28:23 / 29:5, 6

RESPECT

A wise man's speech is respected, and men of common sense are admired as counselors. If you want to be respected and listened to, don't let wisdom and common sense slip away.

Proverbs 3:21, 22 / 10:13 / 14:3

PROMOTION

Don't demand to be promoted as though you were some powerful prince. It is better to wait for a promotion than to be publicly refused and disgraced! Fools will end in shame. But if you promote wisdom, it will promote you. Hold it fast and it will lead you to great honor. Be wise, patient, and hard-working, and you'll be promoted. You'll even stand before kings.

Proverbs 3:35 / 4:7-9 / 22:29 / 25:6, 7, 27

MAN'S BLESSINGS

He who says to the wicked, "You are innocent," shall receive man's curses. He who speaks out fearlessly against sin shall receive blessings. When you bless others, others bless you. Men can give you their favor, honor, respect, fellowship, praise, and appreciation. They can bring you influence, fame, promotion, and riches. But depending on man or your own efforts for these things is a trap. Men are not always true. You could end up losing everything. The only safe way to receive the above blessings is to trust and obey God. He can change men's hearts and cause them to give you these things. But most of all, he'll change you so they'll want to.

*Proverbs 11:24-26 / 12:14 / 21:1 / 22:29 /
24:24, 25 / 29:25, 26*

FAME

Just as it is harmful to eat too much honey, so also it is bad for men to think about all the fame they deserve. If you want to get on the road to fame, accept criticism! It is better to be slow-tempered than famous. In other words, wisdom should come before fame—after all, it is more important than fame. And if you want to be elected to the wise man's hall of fame, again you must profit from constructive criticism.

Proverbs 1:8, 9 / 13:18 / 15:31, 32 / 16:32 / 22:29 / 25:27

INFLUENCE

The good influence of godly citizens causes a city to prosper, but the moral decay of the wicked drives it downhill. Whether you are wise or evil, you will influence the people around you, and they will become like you are. Some men purposely try to influence important people into doing what they want them to by giving them gifts or bribes. And some misuse the influence they have with people to get their own way. But the godly trust God and ask him for what they want.

Proverbs 4:23 / 11:11 / 13:20 / 16:15 / 18:16 / 19:4 / 22:11, 29 / 23:1-3 / 25:6, 7 / 29:25, 26 / 31:31

DIGNITY

God created man in his own image as part of his family. To mock or make fun of another man or even yourself is to mock God. Proverbs were written to teach us how to live—and how to act in every circumstance. God wants us to recognize the high purpose he has for our lives and the greatness he has called us to. We're in his family. He wants us to live like him, to be like him, and to be with him forever.

Proverbs 1:2 / 8:31 / 17:5 / 31:25

154

PART TEN

GOD'S PROTECTION

SAFETY

No real harm befalls the good, but there is constant trouble for the wicked. The path of the godly leads away from evil; he who follows that path is safe. Yes, the Lord is a strong fortress. The godly run to him and are safe. A man is a fool to trust himself! But those who use God's wisdom are safe. Yes, wisdom and common sense will keep them safe from defeat and disaster and from stumbling off the trail. The fear of man is a dangerous trap, but to trust in God means safety.

Proverbs 3:21-26 / 4:27 / 6:20-23 / 11:14 / 12:21 / 16:17 / 17:12 / 18:6, 7, 10, 11 / 19:2 / 21:23 / 22:12 / 24:6 / 28:26 / 29:25

PROTECTION

Every word of God proves true. He defends all who come to him for protection. He is their shield, protecting them and guarding their pathway. Cling to wisdom—she will protect you. Love her and she will guard you. Wisdom and reverence for God give life, happiness, and protection from harm. Yes, God protects the upright.

Proverbs 2:7, 8 / 3:24-26 / 4:6 / 10:29 / 12:21 / 19:23 / 22:12 / 30:5, 24-28

DEFENSE

Don't rob the poor and sick! For the Lord is their defender. If you injure them, he will punish you. And don't try to cheat the defenseless, for their redeemer is strong; he himself will accuse you. The Lord defends the upright but ruins the plans of the wicked. Lying and cheating will get any man into trouble, but honesty is its own defense.

Proverbs 2:7, 8 / 3:24-26 / 4:6 / 12:13 / 18:11 / 20:22 / 21:22 / 22:12, 22, 23 / 23:10, 11/ 29:25 / 30:5

158

REFUGE AND SECURITY

Disaster strikes like a cyclone and the wicked are whirled away. But the good man has a strong anchor. Yes, reverence for God gives a man deep strength; he and his children have a place of refuge and security. The godly have a refuge when they die, but the wicked are crushed by their sins. The rich man thinks he has refuge and security in his riches. And the strong man thinks he has it in strength. What dreamers!

Proverbs 4:27 / 10:25 / 14:26, 32 / 18:10, 11 / 19:23 / 20:28 / 21:22

DELIVERANCE

The good man's goodness delivers him; the evil man's treachery is his undoing. Don't repay evil for evil. Wait for the Lord to handle the matter. For good men will be rescued from harm and danger, but cheaters will be destroyed. And you can also be very sure God will rescue the children of the godly.

Proverbs 4:27 / 11:6, 8, 21 / 16:7 / 20:22 / 24:11, 12

PART ELEVEN

LAW AND JUSTICE

CONFESSING

If you refuse to admit your mistakes, you can never be successful. But if you confess and forsake them, you will get another chance. Your sins are forgiven by God's mercy and truth. And he who values grace and truth is God's friend.

Proverbs 16:6 / 22:11 / 28:13

162

BE FAIR

God rejoices when his people are truthful and fair. In fact, he demands fairness in everything we do. He established this principle. He'll even help you act fairly; so there need be no mistakes. When you are kind, honest, and fair you stand secure. God is more pleased when you are just and fair than when you give him gifts.

Proverbs 16:10-13 / 20:10, 23, 28 / 21:3, 7 / 22:8 / 25:4, 5 / 29:14

MERCY

Those who are merciless and plot evil will not be shown mercy. But those who plan good and show mercy shall be granted mercy. The merciful forgive and are forgiven.

Proverbs 14:22 / 16:6 / 21:7

REWARD

God will reward everyone according to their deeds. But people are not just rewarded after they die, they receive the results of their actions here on earth as well. The wicked reap curses and evil while the godly receive rich and worthwhile rewards. Even if the wicked receive some nice things here on earth, they still won't go unpunished. But the good man's reward is now and forever.

Proverbs 11:18, 21, 31 / 17:26 / 24:11, 12 / 25:21, 22 / 27:18 / 28:10, 20

PUNISHMENT

You can be very sure the evil man and the proud man will not go unpunished forever. The wicked can expect only wrath. And mockers and rebels shall be severely punished. The Lord despises the deeds of the wicked, but loves those who try to be good. If they stop trying, the Lord will punish them; if they rebel against that punishment, they will die. A rebuke to a man of common sense is more effective than a hundred lashes on the back of a rebel.

Proverbs 3:11, 12 / 11:12, 23, 31 / 12:2 / 15:9, 10 / 16:4, 5 / 17:10, 11, 26 / 19:5, 19, 25, 29 / 20:26 / 21:11, 15 / 22:15 / 24:28, 29 / 27:22 / 29:1, 19, 24

REBUKE AND REPROOF

Ignoring sin leads to sorrow; speaking out against sin leads to peace. A wise youth accepts his father's scolding and becomes wiser. To refuse reproof is stupid. If you rebuke a mocker, you will only get a smart retort; yes, he will snarl at you. So don't bother with him; he will only hate you for trying to help him. But a wise man, when rebuked, will love you all the more. He knows that open rebuke is better than hidden love.

Proverbs 9:7-9 / 10:10 / 12:1 / 13:1, 18, 19 / 15:12, 31, 32 / 17:10 / 19:25 / 21:11 / 27:5, 22 / 28:23 / 29:1, 19

RIGHTS

The good man knows and respects the rights of others. The godless don't care. They try again and again to cheat the upright out of their rights. But the upright rise to victory every time and the godless meet calamity.

Proverbs 24:15, 16 / 29:7

DAY OF JUDGMENT

Your riches won't help you on Judgment Day; only righteousness counts then. So since the path of the godly leads to life and life eternal, stay on it and you'll never need to fear death.

Proverbs 11:4 / 12:28

GOVERNMENT

With good men in government, the people rejoice; but with the wicked in power, they groan. Yes, without wise leadership, a nation is in trouble. It is a horrible thing for leaders to do evil. An evil government will oppress its people, hurt the poor, and demand bribes. It favors the wicked and condemns the innocent. Dishonesty and moral rot will cause this government to topple. But with honest, sensible leaders there is stability. A good government and wise leaders are kind, honest, and fair. They are good to the poor, they hate bribes, and they stamp out crime by severe punishment. Yes, good leaders bring peace, safety, and stability to a nation. This government will stand secure and have a long reign.

Proverbs 11:14 / 14:28, 34 / 16:10-15 / 17:26 / 18:5 / 19:10 / 20:26, 28 / 21:1 / 22:8 / 25:4, 5 / 28:2, 15, 16 / 29:2, 4, 12, 14, 16

JUSTICE

Evil men don't understand the importance of justice, but those who follow the Lord are much concerned about it. They know that injustice will destroy a nation. And that the Lord despises those who say that bad is good and good is bad. Justice means punishing evil and rewarding righteousness. Yet some men accept bribes to twist this process. They sentence the poor and let the rich go free. They call the wicked innocent and fine the godly for being good. These men will be cursed by many people and end in disaster. But many blessings will be showered on those who love justice and rebuke sin fearlessly.

Proverbs 8:18, 20 / 13:23 / 14:25 / 17:15, 23, 26 / 21:15 / 22:8 / 24:11, 12, 23-25 / 28:5 / 29:4, 26 / 31:4, 5, 8, 9

AUTHORITIES

I f you have good and honest authorities, rejoice! For authorities such as policemen and other officials prevent crime from running wild. When you complain about these men, you help the spread of wickedness. But when you obey the law and its enforcers you help to fight evil. To evildoers these authorities mean calamity. But to the good they mean justice and safety.

Proverbs 11:14 / 16:14 / 19:12 / 20:2, 26 / 21:15 / 28:4, 7, 9 / 29:2, 18

PART TWELVE
DON'T QUIT

COURAGE

 man's courage can sustain his broken body, but when courage dies, what hope is left?

Proverbs 15:5 / 17:22 / 18:14 / 24:10 / 30:29-31

BOLDNESS

The wicked run away when no one is chasing them! But the godly are bold as lions.

Proverbs 10:10 / 28:1 / 30:29-31

CONFIDENCE

A fool has great confidence. Unfortunately, it is in himself. Putting confidence in yourself alone is like trying to run on a broken foot. But he who respects God and trusts in his Word has strong, well-placed confidence. For every word of God proves true.

Proverbs 3:24-26 / 14:16, 26 / 25:19 / 28:11, 26 / 30:5

176

STRENGTH

T he glory of young men is their physical strength. The glory of old men is their experience and the wisdom experience brings. For the older man has learned that wisdom is mightier than strength. A wise man will conquer a strong man and break down his defenses every time.

Proverbs 10:25 / 12:4 / 14:26 / 17:22 / 20:29 / 21:22, 31 / 24:5 / 30:24-28 / 31:25

PATIENCE

Be patient and you will finally win. An impatient man is a fool. He hates the man who is patient. If you are waiting for something good, continue in patience. For if you become too anxious and lose your patience, you will also lose your hope. And hope that is frustrated makes your heart sick. But if you are patient, you will finally get what you are waiting for.

Proverbs 10:24 / 12:25, 26 / 13:12 / 14:15-17 / 25:15

AMBITION

Ambition and death are alike in this: neither is ever satisfied. Ambition is good as long as your goals are right. The good man is ambitious and works very hard because he loves to give and help others. He also wants to provide well for his family. This ambitious man will prosper. But the greedy man uses his ambition to try and get rich quick. This man will fail. Lazy people lack ambition. Whether their goals are wrong or right they won't reach them, because their hands refuse to work.

Proverbs 7:25 / 10:22 / 13:4 / 21:25, 26 / 23:4, 5 / 27:20 / 28:20

DETERMINATION

A good man's hopes will come true because of his determination. When you lose sight of your goals, you lose your determination and drive. When this happens, you become lazy and full of excuses. The lazy man says, "I can't go to work! If I go outside I might meet a lion in the street and be killed!" A man of determination won't allow himself to get lazy or use excuses. He's determined to reach his goals. He will draw on God's strength and keep going.

Proverbs 4:7 / 10:24 / 14:11, 26 / 22:13 / 24:10, 15, 16 / 25:15 / 28:19

PERSEVERANCE

Perseverance—endurance—brings prosperity. You are a poor specimen if you can't stand the pressure of adversity. Disaster strikes like a cyclone and the wicked are whirled away. But the good man has a strong anchor. Yes, the wicked shall perish; but the godly shall endure everything. The godly, determined person keeps up his courage, never loses his hope, keeps on working, stays cheerful, and never ever quits. Though you trip him up seven times, each time he will rise up again. But one calamity is enough to lay the wicked low.

Proverbs 10:24, 25 / 12:7 / 13:4, 12, 19 / 14:23, 26 / 15:9, 10, 15 / 18:14 / 21:5 / 22:13 / 23:17, 18 / 24:10, 15, 16 / 25:15 / 28:19, 20, 22

THE RIGHT PATH

The good man's path is easy. It leads upward away from evil, leaving hell behind. Those on this path have firm footing, and they enjoy life to the full. The sensible stay on this path and avoid danger. The sinner's path is dark, rocky, and gloomy. It is a wide and pleasant road that seems right but ends in death and destruction. Those on it have strayed away from common sense and have trouble all through life. The man who values his soul will follow the steps of the godly instead. God is a shield to the godly. He protects them and guards their pathway. Listen to advice and you will become aware of the pitfalls on ahead. Check to see where you are going. Watch your step. Stick to the path and be safe. Don't get sidetracked!

Proverbs 2:7, 8, 20-22 / 4:25-27 / 10:9 / 11:5 / 13:9, 14, 15 / 14:12, 15, 16, 22 / 15:19, 21, 24 / 16:17, 25 / 20:24 / 21:16 / 22:5, 6 / 31:2, 3

PART THIRTEEN

YOUR BODY

HEALTH AND VITALITY

Renewed, radiant health and vitality will be given to those who trust and reverence the Lord and turn their back on evil. Yes, wisdom and common sense will fill them with living energy. Here is a list of things that will cause life and health:

- the words of the wise,
- dreams come true,
- gentle words,
- pleasant sights,
- good reports,
- kind words,
- a cheerful heart.

Proverbs 3:7, 8, 21, 22 / 4:21, 22 / 6:14, 15, 21, 22 / 12:18 / 13:12 / 15:4, 16, 30 / 16:24 / 17:22 / 18:14 / 20:12 / 22:22, 23

FOOD

The Lord will not let a good man starve to death. But hunger is good—if it makes you work to satisfy it! A lazy man sleeps soundly—but he goes hungry! Stay awake, work hard, and there will be plenty to eat! The good man eats to live, while the evil man lives to eat. Do you like honey? Don't eat too much of it, or anything else, or it will make you sick. And don't party with drunks and gluttons.

Proverbs 10:3 / 11:24-26 / 12:9 / 13:25 / 15:17 / 16:26 / 17:1 / 18:8, 20 / 19:15, 24 / 20:4, 13, 17 / 22:9 / 23:1-8, 19, 21 / 25:16, 21, 22, 27 / 26:13-15 / 27:7, 18, 12-27 / 30:24-28

185

SLEEP

Learn these lessons and be wise:
    A little extra sleep. Too much sleep will clothe a man with rags.

A little more sleep. A lazy man sticks to his bed like a door to its hinge. Get out of bed when you wake up or you will sleep away your hour of opportunity.

A little folding of the hands to rest. If you love sleep, you will end in poverty. Stay awake, work hard, and you will have plenty. A lazy man sleeps soundly—and he goes hungry.

Proverbs 3:24-26 / 6:6-11 / 10:5 / 19:15 / 20:13 / 23:19-21 / 24:30-34 / 26:13-15

Good Looks

Don't judge yourself or others by good looks. The most important thing is to be good-looking on the inside. A person who is beautiful on the outside and not on the inside is like a fine gold ring in a pig's snout. If you want to know what a person is really like, look at the type of friends they choose.

Proverbs says that kindness makes a person attractive. A good-looking face or body won't last. But if you love and respect God and are kind to others, you'll have a true beauty you will never lose.

Proverbs 11:12 / 19:22 / 22:19 / 31:30

ALCOHOL

Don't party with drunks. Wine gives false courage; hard liquor leads to brawls. What fools men are to let it master them, making them stagger drunkenly down the street! And it is not for leaders to drink wine and whiskey. For if they drink they may forget their duties and be unable to give justice to those who are oppressed.

Proverbs 20:1 / 21:17 / 23:19-21, 29-35 / 31:4-7

MODERATION

Food. Do you like honey? Don't eat too much of it, or it will make you sick.

Fellowship. Don't visit your neighbor too often, or you will wear out your welcome.

Sleep. Too much sleep will clothe a man with rags.

Money. Don't weary yourself trying to get rich. Why waste your time? For riches can disappear as though they had the wings of a bird!

Proverbs 13:25 / 23:1-5, 19-21 / 25:16, 17, 27

CLOTHING

The lazy man is clothed with rags. But the good man is covered with blessings from head to foot. Yes, the diligent have clothes that are beautifully made.

Proverbs 7:10 / 10:6 / 23:19-21 / 27:23-27 / 31:21-24

PART FOURTEEN

THE GOOD LIFE

JOY

I f you want your life filled with joy, let wisdom and truth
enter the very center of your being. If you want your
heart filled with joy, spend your time planning good.
If you want to sing for joy, stay away from evil traps. If you
want learning to be a joy, find a wise teacher. And if you
want to give others joy, be godly and wise.

Proverbs 2:10 / 12:4, 20 / 13:7, 12 / 14:10, 13 / 15:2 / 23:24, 25 / 29:5, 6

LIFE

I would have you learn this great fact: a life of doing right is the wisest life there is. If you live that kind of life, you'll not limp or stumble as you run. Yes, right living brings lasting happiness. The person who tries to live without God gets bored with himself. But the godly man's life is exciting. For only good men enjoy life to the full. Yes, the life of the godly is full of joy, satisfying, long, good, happy, full of light, and easy. But the lives of evil men are destroyed by their own wickedness.

Proverbs 2:10, 20, 21 / 3:1, 2, 16, 17 / 4:4, 10-13, 21-23 / 5:7-9 / 6:20, 23 / 7:2 / 8:35 / 9:6, 11 / 10:2, 17, 27 / 11:7, 19 / 12:28 / 13:6, 9, 12 / 14:14, 30 / 15:19 / 19:16, 18, 23 / 21:8, 21 / 22:4

SINGING

Good men sing for joy!

Proverbs 29:5, 6

PLEASURE

A fool takes pleasure in sinning. But a wise man spends his leisure time wisely. He knows that leisure time is just a small part of his life, a part to be enjoyed with all the rest. A man who loves leisure time becomes poor; wine and luxury are not the way to riches nor the reason for them. Hard work brings prosperity; spending all your time playing around and enjoying leisure time brings poverty.

Proverbs 3:16, 17 / 10:22-24 / 19:28 / 21:17 / 23:19-21 / 28:19

CHEERFULNESS

When a man is gloomy, everything seems to go wrong; when he is cheerful, everything seems right! A cheerful heart does good like medicine, but a broken spirit makes one sick.

Proverbs 14:13 / 15:13, 15 / 17:22 / 25:20

196

FUN AND LAUGHTER

A fool's fun is being bad. He enjoys sinning. Although he may laugh and have fun from time to time, his life is hard and full of trouble. Laughter and a good time cannot mask a heavy heart. When the party is over, the grief remains. But the life of the godly is always exciting. For fun and laughter are always in their hearts.

Proverbs 8:30-32 / 10:23 / 14:13, 14 / 15:9, 13 / 17:22 / 19:28, 29 / 25:20

HAPPINESS

If you want lasting happiness now and forever, live a godly life. Yes, eternal happiness is the hope of good men. An evil man has no lasting happiness. His happiness is based only on this earthly life. The good man is happy and looks forward to continuing happiness, while the wicked can expect only wrath.

Proverbs 3:18 / 4:4 / 8:31-34 / 10:1, 2, 28 / 11:7, 23 / 14:13 / 15:13, 27, 30 / 19:23 / 22:9 / 25:20 / 29:17

PEACE

A dry crust eaten in peace is better than steak every day along with argument and strife. Those who obey God's Word have peace of mind. Yes, wisdom brings peace! When you are peaceful inside yourself you will have peace and make peace around you. An evil man has no peace. His frustrations are heavier than sand and rocks. Therefore he sows strife and discord.

Proverbs 3:16, 17, 30-32 / 6:16-19 / 10:10 / 11:12 / 16:7, 28 / 17:1 / 22:10 / 27:3 / 29:8, 17

CONTENTMENT

A man who is content trusts God and is satisfied when his needs are met. He doesn't waste time trying to get rich. A man who thinks he must be rich to be content shows that he is not content in God. He doesn't trust him. This man is always saying, "I'll be content when I get this certain thing or when this certain event takes place." Don't let your contentment be in things and happenings. When it is, you will forget God if you grow rich and steal if you are too poor.

Proverbs 5:19 / 12:14 / 13:6-9 / 14:14 / 16:26 / 18:20 / 21:5 / 27:7, 20 / 30:8, 9, 15, 16

QUIETNESS

The good shall be granted quietness, both inside and out.

Proverbs 3:16, 17 / 14:22

LONGER DAYS

"I, wisdom, will make the hours of your day more profitable and the years of your life more fruitful." Reverence, for God is what adds hours to each day, so how can the wicked expect to accomplish as much as the good?"

Proverbs 9:11 / 10:27 / 14:30

202

VICTORY

If you need a victory, prepare yourself to do the task and do it well. But trust God for the outcome. He'll see to it that the wicked lose and righteous are victorious.

If you are looking for victory in friendly competition or self-improvement, practice hard and trust God. Then if you are patient and never quit, you will finally win.

Proverbs 12:7 / 21:5, 18, 22, 31 / 23:17, 18 / 24:15, 16 / 25:15

CELEBRATE

Celebrate with the good when good prevails.

Celebrate your godly friends' successes,
the things that make them rejoice—

a victory, an accomplishment, or even a marriage.

Celebrate when good men gain positions of authority.

And celebrate when God's wisdom helps you avoid evil.

Proverbs 5:18 / 11:20 / 28:12 / 29:2, 6

PART FIFTEEN

YOUR FUTURE

GOALS

Have two main goals: wisdom and common sense. Let every other goal line up with these. Wisdom is the main pursuit of sensible men, but a fool's goals are at the ends of the earth. Wise men look and think ahead. They gather the facts and then map out their goals. When you do this, make sure you set reasonable goals, goals that you know can be reached. A man fails when he tries to do things too quickly. Don't brag about your goals—wait and see what happens. Once you have set your goals, look straight ahead and don't sidetrack. But the most important thing to remember is to let the Lord direct your steps. Make sure your goals are his goals, then trust him to bring them about. Man makes plans, but God causes things to happen in his own way.

Proverbs 3:21-26 / 4:25-27 / 6:16-19 / 8:17, 21, 27-29 / 13:4, 16 / 14:8 / 17:24 / 19:21 / 20:18, 24 / 24:3, 4 / 27:1 / 28:20, 22

YOUR TIME

A wise youth makes good use of all his time. It is a shame to see someone sleeping or wasting away their hour of opportunity. So don't waste your time following some get-rich-quick scheme, oversleeping, or just fooling around. Hard work means prosperity; only a fool idles away his time.

Proverbs 9:11 / 10:5, 22, 27 / 12:11, 14, 17 / 13:4, 16 / 21:25, 26 / 23:4, 5 / 24:3, 4

HOPE

The wicked man's fears will all come true, and so
will the good man's hopes. When an evil man
dies, his hopes all perish, for they are based upon
this earthly life. Hope deferred makes the heart sick; but
when dreams come true at last, there is life and joy. The
hope of good men is eternal happiness; the hopes of evil
men are all in vain.

Proverbs 10:24, 28 / 11:7, 23 / 13:12 / 15:15 / 18:14 / 21:5 / 23:17, 18 / 24:13, 14 / 28:3 / 29:20

GUIDANCE

Since the Lord is directing our steps, why try to understand everything that happens along the way? Trust the Lord completely; don't ever trust yourself alone. In everything you do, put God first, and he will direct you and crown your efforts with success.

Proverbs 2:7-9 / 3:4-6 / 6:20-23 / 10:8 / 11:3, 5 / 13:14 / 14:15, 16 / 16:1, 3, 9 / 19:21 / 20:24 / 21:1, 16 / 22:3 / 26:3

YOUR DREAMS

The godly have wonderful futures ahead of them. Looking forward to the great things God has in store for you is often called dreaming. These pleasant sights give happiness and health and encourage you to keep going. But don't just dream—commit your work to the Lord and get on with it. And when your dream comes true at last, there will be life and joy.

Proverbs 11:23 / 13:4, 12 / 14:8 / 15:30 / 16:3 / 19:21 / 23:17, 18

YOUR FUTURE

PAST   PRESENT   FUTURE

An evil man has no future; his light will be snuffed out. So don't envy him, for only the godly have wonderful futures ahead of them. Yes, when you enjoy becoming wise, a very bright future awaits you.

Proverbs 21:20 / 23:17, 18 / 24:13, 14, 19, 20

DECISIONS

Rules for making the right decision:
- A good man is guided by his honesty. Always go the way of honesty.
- Don't decide before knowing all the facts. That is stupidity.
- Don't rush your decision. A cautious man avoids danger.
- Don't believe everything you are told. A prudent man makes sure.
- And most importantly, don't be conceited and sure of your own decisions. Put God first, and he will show you how to make the right decision every time.

Proverbs 2:9 / 3:4-8 / 11:3, 5 / 14:15, 16 / 16:19 / 18:13 / 21:21

PLANS

We can make our plans, but the final outcome is in God's hands. So count on God to direct you right from the start. Men make plans, but God causes things to happen in his own way. And don't go ahead with your plans without the advice of others. Plans go wrong with too few advisors; many advisors bring success. It is pleasant to see plans develop. That is why fools refuse to give them up even when they are wrong.

Proverbs 6:16-19 / 12:20 / 13:16, 19 / 14:8, 22 / 15:22 / 16:1, 9, 30 / 19:21 / 20:18, 24 / 21:31 / 22:12 / 27:1, 12 / 30:32

PLANNING GOOD

SURPRISE

Those who plot evil will wander away and be lost, but those who plan good will be granted mercy and quietness. Deceit fills the hearts that are plotting evil; joy fills the hearts that are planning good.

Proverbs 6:16-19 / 12:20 / 14:22 / 16:30 / 30:32

ANOTHER CHANCE

The man who is often reproved but refuses to accept criticism will suddenly be broken and never have another chance. Yes, a man who refuses to admit his mistakes can never be successful. But if he confesses and forsakes them, he gets another chance.

Proverbs 10:17 / 28:13 / 29:1

DESIRES

Desires can be good. But the wrong desires can get you into trouble. The good man desires to help others and do right. He only desires things that line up with his godly life. His desires are good. The lazy man desires many things but his hands refuse to work. His desires would be useful if they caused him to get a job. An evil man's desires are sin. He wants what belongs to others and his constant desire is to get rich quick. These desires are wrong and end in failure. So don't let your desires get out of hand. Stay away from sin and the desires of the wicked.

Proverbs 7:25 / 12:12 / 13:4 / 16:26 / 21:25, 26 / 24:19, 20 / 27:7 / 28:20, 22

PART SIXTEEN

WORK AND MONEY

INHERITANCE

When a good man dies, he leaves an inheritance to his grandchildren. When a sinner dies, his wealth is stored up for the godly. A father can give his children homes and riches, but the best inheritance is godliness. Yes, it is a wonderful heritage to have honest parents.

Proverbs 13:22 / 17:2 / 19:14 / 20:7

SAVING

he wise man saves for the future, but the foolish man spends whatever he gets. The wise also save by watching for bargains. Either way, the wealth of the sensible person grows. But remember, it is possible to give away and become richer! It is also possible to hold on too tightly and lose everything.

Proverbs 3:27, 28 / 11:24, 25 / 13:11 / 21:20 / 31:16-18

PAYING YOUR BILLS

Don't withhold repayment of your debts. Don't say, "some other time," if you can pay now. Remember, just as the rich rule the poor, so the borrower is servant to the lender.

Proverbs 3:27, 28 / 22:7

OPPORTUNITY

A wise youth makes hay while the sun shines, but
what a shame to see a lad who sleeps away his
hour of opportunity. The diligent man makes good
use of everything he finds. Yes, he takes advantage of
every opportunity. A fool will ruin his chances by passing
up opportunities and then blame his failure on the Lord.
The intelligent man is always open to new opportunities. In
fact, he looks for them.

Proverbs 10:5 / 12:27 / 18:15 / 19:3 / 22:13, 29 / 26:13-15

PROFIT

Any enterprise is built by wise planning, becomes strong through common sense, and profits wonderfully by keeping abreast of the facts.
Work brings profit, but talk brings poverty!

Proverbs 9:11 / 14:23 / 15:31, 32 / 24:3, 4

GIVING

Honor the Lord by giving him the first part of all your income, and he will cause everything you do to multiply and succeed. The good man's earnings advance the cause of righteousness. The evil man squanders his on sin. When you give to the poor you are lending to the Lord—and he pays wonderful interest on your loan! It is possible to give away and become richer. It is also possible to hold on too tightly and lose everything. Yes, the generous man shall be rich! By watering others, he waters himself. The godly love to give!

Proverbs 3:9, 10 / 10:16 / 11:24, 25 / 12:12 / 13:7 / 14:21, 31 / 15:25 / 17:5 / 19:6, 7, 17 / 21:3, 13, 25, 26 / 22:9 / 28:27 / 29:14 / 31:19, 20

GIFTS

A gift does wonders; it will bring you before men of importance! It will also silence an angry man. Yes, a gift works like magic. Whoever uses it will prosper. But remember it is wrong to give or accept a bribe or gift to twist justice. One who doesn't give the gift he promised is like a cloud blowing over a desert without dropping any rain. God loathes the gifts of evil men, especially if they are trying to bribe him! He is more pleased when we are just and fair than when we give him gifts.

Proverbs 15:8 / 17:8, 23 / 18:16 / 21:3, 14, 27 / 23:6-8 / 25:14 / 31:19, 20

SUCCESS

Here are the keys to success:
1. Love wisdom.
2. Live a godly life.
3. Obey God's Word.
4. Put God first in everything you do.
5. Commit your work to the Lord.
6. Get and follow wise counsel.
7. Admit and forsake your mistakes.
8. Work hard.

And remember, steady going brings success. Trying to make it happen overnight will just end in trouble.

Proverbs 3:6, 9, 10 / 9:11 / 11:10, 28 / 12:3, 11, 24 / 13:4, 13 / 14:11, 12 / 15:22 / 16:3 / 19:8, 10 / 21:5 / 22:29 / 23:4, 5 / 24:3, 4, 15, 16 / 27:23-27 / 28:12, 13, 19, 20, 25, 28

SPENDING MONEY

The good man's earnings advance the cause of righteousness. The evil man squanders his on sin. Yes, a man who loves pleasure will spend all his money on it and become poor. This foolish man won't even budget the money he gets. But the diligent man makes good use of every dollar. The wise man saves for the future, but the foolish man spends whatever he gets.

Proverbs 3:9, 10, 27, 28 / 10:16 / 11:24, 26 / 12:26, 27 / 13:11 / 16:11 / 21:17, 20 / 28:5 / 31:16-18

TALENT AND ABILITY

Doing a job for which you have talent and ability is satisfying. And an employer rejoices in a worker who knows what he is doing. But just because you are good and talented, don't start thinking that you are beyond instruction or correction. And don't think that you are too good to do a lesser job. If your ability goes to your head in this way, your boss would be better off hiring an untrained apprentice.

Proverbs 11:9 / 12:9 / 14:35 / 18:20 / 26:10

LOANS

Be sure you know a person well before you vouch for his credit! Better refuse than suffer later. And even if you know the person well, it is still poor judgment to countersign another's note, to become responsible for his debts. Since you know this to be true, it would be unfair for you to expect others to countersign your debts. It is better to wait until you can do it yourself. And that becomes a good safeguard. Borrowing money to buy a lot of things you can't afford is like trying to get rich quick; it ends in trouble. So use credit wisely and remember, just as the rich rule the poor, so the borrower is servant to the lender.

Proverbs 6:1-5 / 11:15 / 17:13, 18 / 19:17 / 20:16 / 22:7, 26, 27

INCOME

When you receive an income, honor God by giving him the first part. Then he will cause the rest of it to go a lot further. Secondly, pay your bills. Never put them off when you can pay them now. It is also important to have your basic needs paid for. Such as food, clothing, and shelter. Now that you have done all that, it is also very important to handle the rest of your income wisely. A wise man saves for the future. Investing your money is another wise thing to do. Next, spend some money. The godly are to enjoy life to the full. But do it wisely, and don't spend over what you planned to. Two other very important things to remember are offerings and giving to the poor. A good man's earnings should advance the cause of righteousness.

Proverbs 3:9, 10 / 10:16 / 11:16, 18, 24, 25 / 12:11, 27 / 13:4, 11 / 14:4, 23 / 21:20 / 22:9 / 27:18, 23-27 / 28:8, 19, 20

GAIN

A little gained honestly is better than great wealth gotten by dishonest means. Some men enjoy cheating, but the cake they buy with such ill-gotten gain will turn to gravel in their mouths. Yes, it will bring grief to a whole family. Quick wealth is not a blessing in the end. And dishonest gain will never last, so why take the risk?

Proverbs 10:16 / 13:11 / 14:23 / 15:27 / 16:8 / 20:17, 21 / 21:6 / 22:1 / 28:6, 8, 18

230

EMPLOYEES

A faithful employee is as refreshing as a cool day in the hot summertime. But a lazy fellow is a pain to his employers—like smoke in their eyes or vinegar that sets the teeth on edge.

Proverbs 10:26 / 12:24 / 14:35 / 16:26 / 22:29 / 25:13, 19 / 26:10 / 27:18 / 28:19 / 30:10

BUYING AND SELLING

When a dishonest man has something to sell, he holds onto it until he can get the highest possible price. But when he's buying something he says "utterly worthless" as he haggles over the price. Then afterward he brags about the bargain he got. The Lord demands fairness in every business deal. He established this principle. So when you are selling something, let it go for a fair price. When you are buying, look for a good deal but also consider the necessary profit of the vendor.

Proverbs 11:26 / 13:2 / 16:11 / 18:16 / 20:14, 17 / 24:27 / 27:23-27 / 31:16-18

INVESTING YOUR MONEY

Don't get involved with investment schemes that claim they will make you rich quickly. They are evil and really lead to poverty. Go inspect your investment before committing yourself. Know all the facts and make sure you check its past record. For putting confidence in something unreliable is like chewing with a sore tooth. And after you have made an investment, follow it closely.

Here is a reliable investment tip: When you give to people in need, you are lending to the Lord—and he pays wonderful interest on every investment.

Proverbs 3:9, 10 / 10:16 / 14:4 / 15:22, 27 / 19:17 / 25:19 / 27:23-27 / 28:20, 22 / 31:16-18

TRUE RICHES

Some rich people are poor, and some poor people have great wealth. The man who knows right from wrong and has good judgment and common sense is happier than the man who is immensely rich! For such wisdom is far more valuable than precious jewels. Nothing else compares with it. The Lord's blessing is our greatest wealth. All our work adds nothing to it! If you must choose, take righteousness rather than great riches; for to be loved by God is better than silver and gold. Riches won't help you on Judgment Day; only righteousness counts then. The evil man gets rich for the moment, but the good man's reward lasts forever.

Proverbs 3:13-17 / 10:22 / 11:4, 18 / 13:7 / 22:1, 2

WEALTH

Trust in your money and down you go! Trust in God and flourish! Don't weary yourself trying to get rich. Why waste your time? For riches can disappear as though they had the wings of a bird! The rich man thinks of his wealth as an impregnable defense, a high wall of safety. What a dreamer! If a godly man is rich, his wealth will be accompanied by wisdom, humility, and respect for the Lord. You cannot tell if a man is godly by whether he is rich or poor. The rich and poor are alike to the Lord. So don't treat rich people with favor and the poor with disrespect. The right way to riches is through hard work and loving wisdom. Wisdom distributes unending riches. Those who love and follow wisdom are indeed wealthy. It fills their treasuries. Riches don't come overnight. And a man who loves pleasure becomes poor.

Proverbs 3:13-17 / 8:17-21 / 10:3, 6, 22 / 11:4, 18, 24, 25, 28 /
12:11 / 13:4, 7, 11, 22 / 14:20 / 15:6, 16 / 16:8, 16, 19 /
18:11 / 19:1, 4, 14 / 21:5, 17 / 22:1, 2, 4, 7 /
23:4, 5 / 24:19, 20 / 27:23-27 /
28:6, 11, 19, 20, 22, 25 / 30:7-9

WORK

Hard work means prosperity; only a fool idles away his time. Work brings profit; talk brings poverty. Work hard and become a leader; be lazy and never succeed. If you love sleep, you will end in poverty. Stay awake, work hard, and there will be plenty to eat! Do you know a hard-working man? He shall be successful and stand before kings! Lazy people want much and get little, while the wealth of a hard-working man grows and grows.

Proverbs 6:6-11 / 10:4, 5, 22, 26 / 12:9, 11, 14, 24 / 13:4, 11 / 14:11, 23 / 16:26, 27 / 20:4, 13 / 21:5, 25, 26 / 22:13, 29 / 24:30-34 / 26:10, 13-15 / 28:19 / 31:17, 27

EXPERIENCE

The glory of old people is their experience. And many of their experiences have brought them wisdom. So slow down, and don't rely so much on your strength. Listen to experience and don't despise it.

Proverbs 14:35 / 20:29 / 23:22

THANKFULNESS

I f you have good things and a good life, make sure you thank God who gave them to you.

Proverbs 20:12, 24 / 21:3

238

PART SEVENTEEN

TEACHING

TEACHING OTHERS

Everyone enjoys teaching others. But only men with common sense will be chosen and admired as teachers. Helping others by sharing with them what you have learned satisfies like a good meal. Don't waste your breath on someone who doesn't want to learn from you. He will despise even the wisest things you say. If someone wants to know something that you know, they will ask you. When they do, speak the truth and be kind. A pleasant teacher is best. A curse on those who lead astray the godly. But if you encourage others to do good you will be given a worthwhile reward.

Proverbs 10:13 / 15:7, 23 / 16:21 / 18:20 / 20:5 / 22:6 / 23:9 / 24:7 / 28:10 / 31:26

GIVING ADVICE

It is wonderful to give good advice and to be able to say the right thing at the right time! Timely advice is as lovely as gold apples in a silver basket. The advice of a wise man should refresh like water from a mountain spring. It should be as pleasant as perfume. The upright speak what is helpful and encouraging; the wicked speak rebellion. A godly man gives good advice, but a rebel lacks common sense. Sometimes it seems easier not to give some very necessary advice. But open rebuke is better than hidden love! And the wounds from a friend are better than kisses from an enemy!

Proverbs 10:21, 31, 32 / 12:25 / 13:14, 15 / 15:7, 23 / 18:20 / 23:9 / 25:11 / 27:5, 6, 9 / 28:10 / 29:19 / 31:26

SPEAKING PROVERBS

As you read wise sayings, explore the depths of meaning in each nugget of truth. As you learn what they mean you will be able to speak them accurately to others. A rebel will misapply an illustration so that its point will no more be felt than a thorn in the hand of a drunkard. In the mouth of a fool a proverb becomes as useless as a paralyzed leg.

Proverbs 1:5, 6 / 15:23 / 25:11 / 26:7, 9 / 31:26

SHARE YOUR WISDOM

As you listen to wise advice and follow it closely you will be able to pass it on to others. Trust in the Lord, learn and believe his Word. For God expects you to share it with others.

Proverbs 22:17-21

LEADERSHIP

If you want to become a leader, you must work hard. Lazy men never succeed. If you become a leader before you are ready, your short term of leadership will end in disaster. Trust God and he will prepare you for the job. First of all, you must be wise. And your right to lead will depend on your fairness. In order to bring stability to what you are leading you must be kind, honest, and sensible. But most importantly, you must learn to use God's help to lead. Use his strength and trust him to direct your thoughts and guide your decisions. If you do this, there will be no reasons for mistakes. And the people you lead will rejoice in your leadership.

Proverbs 1:5, 6 / 8:14-16 / 11:14 / 12:24 / 13:20 / 16:10, 12, 21 / 17:2 / 19:10 / 20:28 / 21:1 / 22:8 / 28:2, 15 / 29:2, 4, 12, 14, 16 / 31:4, 5

244

PART EIGHTEEN

AND OTHER THINGS

ANIMALS

A good man is concerned for the welfare of his animals, but even the kindness of godless men is cruel.

Proverbs 12:10

246

GOOD NEWS

Good news from far away is like cold water to the thirsty.

Proverbs 25:25

THE
VIRTUOUS WOMAN

The virtuous woman gets up before dawn to prepare breakfast for her household, and she plans the day's work for her servant girls. She goes out to inspect a field and buys it. With her own hands she plants a vineyard. She is energetic, a hard worker, and watches for bargains. She works far into the night! She sews for the poor and generously helps those in need. She has no fear of winter for her household, for she has made warm clothes for all of them. Her own clothing is beautifully made—a purple gown of pure linen. She makes belted linen garments to sell to the merchants. She is a woman of strength and dignity, and she has no fear of old age. When she speaks, her words are wise, and kindness is the rule for everything she says. She watches carefully all that goes on throughout her household, and she is never lazy. Her children stand and bless her; so does her husband. He praises her with these words: "There are many fine women in the world, but you are the best of all!" Charm can be deceptive and beauty doesn't last, but a woman who fears and honors God shall be greatly praised.

Proverbs 11:16, 22 /
12:4 / 14:1 / 19:13, 14 /
21:9, 19 / 25:24 / 27:15 / 31:10-31

JESUS THE WISE

When Jesus was twelve years old he went with Joseph and Mary to Jerusalem. On the way back to Nazareth, Jesus was missing from the group, and after a while Joseph and Mary realized he was not with any of their friends. Very worried, they returned to Jerusalem and found Jesus at the temple, talking with the great religious teachers and asking them questions. The teachers were amazed that a twelve-year-old boy could know so much.

This story, found in Luke's Gospel, ends with the statement that Jesus "grew both tall and wise." While he was growing up physically, his knowledge of God and man's dealings with God was also growing.

Jesus is known to Christians as their Savior and Lord, but was also well-known to people of his day as a wise teacher. Usually when someone spoke to him they called him "Teacher," or "Rabbi," which means the same thing. Like other teach ers of his day he gathered disciples—learners—around him and answered the questions of people who needed advice. He taught his disciples in private and taught publicly in the open air, in synagogues, and in the temple. The people liked his teaching, and even his enemies could see that he was a great teacher.

Just as Solomon is shown to be wiser than anyone in the Old Testament, Jesus the teacher is wiser than anyone in the New Testament. Like Solomon's sayings, Jesus' words of wisdom were written down.

Solomon's sayings in the Book of Proverbs tell us how to treat other human beings in the right way. Jesus also had much to say about how to treat others, especially in his famous Sermon on the Mount, found in Matthew 5-7. In this sermon he talked about such subjects as keeping promises, getting revenge, serving God, loving one's enemies, helping the poor, accumulating possessions, and worrying. These are the same subjects that Solomon and other famous wise men talked about in their sayings. "Don't criticize, and then you won't be criticized" is a wise statement by Jesus that sounds like some of Solomon's proverbs. Many of these kinds of sayings by Jesus are admired even by people who do not believe in God.

Jesus did more than say wise things. Christians have always believed that Jesus actually *was* God's wisdom, the wisdom that is described in Proverbs 8:12-36. According to these verses, wisdom existed even before the world was created and was with God as he made the universe. The New Testament says that Christ existed with God through all eternity, before the world was made (John 1:1-3). So Jesus Christ was not only a wise man, but, more importantly, he was himself the wisdom of God in human form.

If we love and trust Jesus we are, at the same time, loving and trusting the wisdom of God. When we do this, Jesus' wisdom becomes ours. Because we have this wisdom, we can understand many things about ourselves and about God, things that unbelievers cannot understand.

Jesus, the wisdom of God, was much more than a teacher. He healed people and worked many miracles to show the power of God. His main purpose in the world was to save us from our sins and give us everlasting life. But he also left to his disciples many wise sayings, sayings that they wrote down in the Gospels and passed on to us. Because they wrote down Jesus' wise words, we can know how the Son of God wanted his followers to live. And we can continually ask God for more wisdom, because the Bible promises us that those who believe in Jesus, God's wisdom, can have all the wisdom they need.

250

PROFILES FROM PROVERBS

A wise man is some-one who . . .

listens to others (12:15)

is always thinking ahead (13:16)

knows how to hold his tongue (10:14)

is glad to be taught (10:8)

loves someone who gives constructive criticism (9:7-8)

saves for the future (21:20)

stays cool when he is insulted (12:16)

is eager to make hay while the sun shines (10:5)

learns lessons from nature (6:6)

accepts the advice of older people (13:1)

has other wise people as friends (13:20)

is cautious and avoids danger (14:16)

is praised for his wisdom (14:24)

knows how to control his temper (14:29)

is hungry for the truth (15:14)

speaks carefully and persuasively (16:23)

speaks few words (17:27)

overlooks insults (19:11)

obeys the law (28:7)

makes his parents happy (29:3)

A foolish man is someone who . . .

idles away his time (12:11)

tries to live without God's help and falls flat on his face (10:8)

blurts out everything he knows (10:14)

says bad things about other people (10:18)

provokes his family to anger and resentment (11:29)

thinks he needs no advice (12:15)

is quick-tempered (12:16)

puts his foolishness on display (12:23)

doesn't think ahead (13:16)

won't face facts (14:8)

won't listen to his father's advice (15:5)

lets his mouth get him into many fights (18:6-7)

repeats his mistakes over and over (26:11)

trusts himself instead of God (28:26)

quarrels with his neighbors (11:12)

spends whatever he gets and doesn't save anything (21:20)

252

What wisdom is like . . .

it is available to everyone (1:20)

it is a gift from God (2:6)

it saves a man from evil women (2:16-17)

it is more valuable than jewels (3:13-15)

it gives peace and a long life (3:16-17)

it brings honor and riches (3:16-17)

it walks hand in hand with good judgment (8:12)

it hates pride and arrogance (8:13)

it is rooted in the fear of God (9:10)

it makes the hours of the day profitable (9:11)

it comes easily to anyone with good sense (14:6)

it is mightier than strength (24:5)

What a generous man is like . . .

he honors the Lord by giving him the first part of his income (3:9-10)

he uses his earnings to advance the cause of righteousness (10:16)

he gives to others, but still gets richer (11:24-25)

he doesn't hold too tightly to what he possesses (11:24-25)

he doesn't hoard what he has (11:26)

he is not jealous of what others have (12:12)

he does favors for others (19:6)

he has many friends (19:6)

he pleases the Lord by helping the poor (19:17)

he is just and fair (21:3)

he feeds the hungry (22:9)

he has his own needs taken care of (28:27)

What makes a good leader . . .

he hates dishonesty and bribes (28:16)

he leads with the help of wisdom (8:16)

he leads with fairness (16:12)

he rejoices in having faithful servants (14:35)

he has God's help so he can judge fairly (16:10)

he rejoices when people are truthful and fair (16:13)

253

he weighs evidence carefully
(20:8)

he stamps out crime by severe
punishment (20:26)

he gives stability to the country
(29:4)

he is fair to the poor (29:14)

he does not oppress the people
(28:16)

What a good friend is like . . .

he is always loyal (17:17)

he sticks closer than a brother
(18:24)

he does not abandon you in time
of need (19:7)

he criticizes for your own good
(but in a loving way, not to be
mean) (27:6)

he never gives up on you (27:10)

he gives good advice (12:26)

he overlooks mistakes (17:9)

he is honest about his true
feelings (20:6)

A lazy man . . .

sleeps his life away (6:9)

always has an excuse for himself
(22:13)

is destroyed by poverty (6:11)

is a pain to the people he works
for (10:26)

never succeeds (12:24)

wants a lot but gets little (13:4)

has trouble all through life (15:19)

is more eager to get than to give
(21:25-26)

thinks he is smarter than anyone
else (26:16)

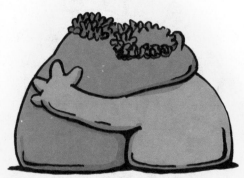

A hard worker . . .

doesn't need someone to make
him work (6:6-7)

doesn't oversleep (6:6-11)

gets rich (10:4)

puts God first in everything (3:6)

consults others when making plans (15:22)

loves wisdom (19:8)

can admit he makes mistakes and doesn't repeat them (28:13)

works steadily (21:5)

trusts God (28:25)

is not too proud to get his hands dirty (12:9)

brings many blessings (12:14)

becomes a leader (12:24)

prospers (13:4)

makes a profit (14:23)

doesn't go hungry (16:26)

works even when conditions are bad (20:4)

works steadily (21:5)

is energetic (31:17)

carefully watches over everything he is in charge of (31:27)

A man is successful when he . . .

obeys God's Word (13:13)

works hard (12:24)

commits his work to the Lord (16:3)

seeks something in life besides pleasure (21:17)

is humble (22:4)

accepts criticism (13:18)

speaks gentle words and doesn't gripe (15:4)

An angry man . . .

is quick-tempered (12:16)

can't control his tongue (13:3)

255

doesn't keep his cool when insulted (12:16)

is a fool (12:16)

has no self-control (13:3)

hates a man who has patience (14:17)

doesn't know that anger causes mistakes (14:29)

causes quarrels (15:1)

bears his own penalties (19:19)

endangers others (22:24-25)

is as defenseless as a city with broken walls (25:28)

gets into all kinds of trouble (29:22)

holds his temper in (29:11)

keeps his head when he is insulted (12:16)

A man with self-control . . .

does not act in anger (14:29)

can control his tongue (13:3)

is better off than someone who controls an army (16:32)

is not defenseless (25:28)

puts an end to fights (15:18)

What happens to a proud man . . .

he ends in shame (11:2)

he may end up starving (12:9)

he has his possessions destroyed (15:25)

he ends up punished for his pride (16:5)

he is worse off than a poor person (16:19)

he brings financial trouble on himself (6:3)

he finds himself in many arguments (13:10)

256

he suffers a great fall (16:18)

he ends up worse off than a fool (26:12)

We get into trouble when we . . .

can't keep our mouths shut (21:23)

are suspicious of everyone else (17:20)

don't listen to wisdom (1:26)

get involved in the finances of strangers (6:1)

blurt out whatever is on our minds (10:14)

don't have wise leaders (11:14)

tell lies (12:13)

behave wickedly (12:21)

pay no heed to God's Word (13:13)

communicate badly (13:17)

are lazy (15:19)

boast and argue (17:19)

lose our tempers (29:22)

What happens to liars . . .

they will be suddenly destroyed (6:15)

they will be caught (19:9)

they have other liars as companions (17:4)

they come to shame (13:5)

they are exposed in time (12:19)

The benefits of living God's way . . .

boldness (28:1)

a wonderful future (23:17-18)

a good reputation (22:1)

an attractive personality (19:22)

a pure heart (17:3)

peace with our worst enemies (16:7)

an easy path in life (15:19)

strength, security, and shelter (14:26)

praise from others (14:24)

quietness (14:22)

appreciation (13:15)

protection from harm (12:21)

prosperity (12:11)

admiration (12:8)

a reward that lasts forever (11:18)

eternal happiness (10:28)

hopes will come true (10:24)

a firm hold in life (10:9)

approval from the Lord (8:35)

knowledge and understanding (8:12)

promotion to honor (3:35)

direction from God (3:6)

a long life (3:16-17)

peace (3:16-17)

pleasure (3:16-17)

health and vitality (3:7-8)

a life full of joy (2:10)

good sense (2:7-8)

being filled with living energy (3:22)

safety from defeat and disaster (3:23)

freedom from fear (3:24-26)

success (3:6)

unending riches (8:18)

all our needs are supplied (28:27)

THE BOOK OF PROVERBS

1 These are the proverbs of King Solomon of Israel, David's son:

²He wrote them to teach his people how to live— how to act in every circumstance, ³for he wanted them to be understanding, just and fair in everything they did. ⁴"I want to make the simple-minded wise!" he said. "I want to warn young men about some problems they will face. ⁵⁻⁶I want those already wise to become the wiser and become leaders by exploring the depths of meaning in these nuggets of truth."

⁷⁻⁹How does a man become wise? The first step is to trust and reverence the Lord! Only fools refuse to be taught. Listen to your father and mother. What you learn from them will stand you in good stead; it will gain you many honors.

¹⁰If young toughs tell you, "Come and join us"—turn your back on them! ¹¹"We'll hide and rob and kill," they say. ¹²"Good or bad, we'll treat them all alike. ¹³And the loot we'll get! All kinds of stuff! ¹⁴Come on, throw in your lot with us; we'll split with you in equal shares."

¹⁵Don't do it, son! Stay far from men like that, ¹⁶for crime is their way of life, and murder is their specialty. ¹⁷When a bird sees a trap being set, it stays away, ¹⁸but not these men; they trap themselves! They lay a booby trap for their own lives. ¹⁹Such is the fate of all who live by violence and murder. They will die a violent death.

²⁰Wisdom shouts in the streets for a hearing. ²¹She calls out to the crowds along Main Street, and to the judges in their courts, and to everyone in all the land: ²²"You simpletons!" she cries. "How long will you go on being fools? How

long will you scoff at wisdom and fight the facts? ²³Come here and listen to me! I'll pour out the spirit of wisdom upon you, and make you wise. ²⁴I have called you so often but still you won't come. I have pleaded, but all in vain. ²⁵For you have spurned my counsel and reproof. ²⁶Some day you'll be in trouble, and I'll laugh! Mock me, will you?—I'll mock you! ²⁷When a storm of terror surrounds you, and when you are engulfed by anguish and distress, ²⁸then I will not answer your cry for help. It will be too late though you search for me ever so anxiously.

²⁹"For you closed your eyes to the facts and did not choose to reverence and trust the Lord, ³⁰and you turned your back on me, spurning my advice. ³¹That is why you must eat the bitter fruit of having your own way, and experience the full terrors of the pathway you have chosen. ³²For you turned away from me—to death; your own complacency will kill you. Fools! ³³But all who listen to me shall live in peace and safety, unafraid."

2 Every young man who listens to me and obeys my instructions will be given wisdom and good sense. ³⁻⁵Yes, if you want better insight and discernment, and are searching for them as you would for lost money or hidden treasure, then wisdom will be given you, and knowledge of God himself; you will soon learn the importance of reverence for the Lord and of trusting him.

⁶For the Lord grants wisdom! His every word is a treasure of knowledge and understanding. ⁷⁻⁸He grants good sense to the godly—his saints. He is their shield, protecting them and guarding their pathway. ⁹He shows how to distinguish right from wrong, how to find the right decision every time. ¹⁰For wisdom and truth will enter the very center of your being, filling your life with joy. ¹¹⁻¹³You will be given the sense to stay away from evil men who want you to be their partners in crime—men who turn from God's ways to walk down dark and evil paths, ¹⁴and exult in doing wrong, for they thoroughly enjoy their sins. ¹⁵Everything they do is crooked and wrong.

¹⁶⁻¹⁷Only wisdom from the Lord can save a man from the flattery of prostitutes; these girls have abandoned their husbands and flouted the laws of God. ¹⁸Their houses lie along the road to death and hell. ¹⁹The men who enter them are doomed. None of these men will ever be the same again.

²⁰Follow the steps of the godly instead, and stay on the right path, ²¹for only good men enjoy life to the full; ²²evil men lose the good things they might have had, and they themselves shall be destroyed.

3 My son, never forget the things I've taught you. If you want a long and satisfying life, closely follow my instructions. ³Never tire of loyalty and kindness. Hold these virtues tightly. Write them deep within your heart. ⁴⁻⁵If you want favor with both God and man, and a reputation for good judgment and common sense, then trust the Lord completely; don't ever trust yourself. ⁶In everything you do, put God first, and he will direct you and crown your efforts with success.

⁷⁻⁸Don't be conceited, sure of your own wisdom. Instead, trust and reverence the Lord, and turn your back on evil; when you do that, then you will be given renewed health and vitality.

⁹⁻¹⁰Honor the Lord by giving him the first part of all your income, and he will fill your barns with wheat and barley and overflow your wine vats with the finest wines.

¹¹⁻¹²Young man, do not resent it when God chastens and corrects you, for his punishment is proof of his love. Just as a father punishes a son he delights in to make him better, so the Lord corrects you.

¹³⁻¹⁵The man who knows right from wrong and has good judgment and common sense is happier than the man who is immensely rich! For such wisdom is far more valuable than precious jewels. Nothing else compares with it.

¹⁶⁻¹⁷Wisdom gives: A long, good life, riches, honor, pleasure, peace.

¹⁸Wisdom is a tree of life to those who eat her fruit; happy is the man who keeps on eating it.

¹⁹The Lord's wisdom founded the earth; his understanding established all the universe and space. ²⁰The deep fountains of the earth were broken open by his knowledge, and the skies poured down rain.

²¹Have two goals: wisdom: that is, knowing and doing right: and common sense. Don't let them slip away, ²²for they fill you with living energy, and bring you honor and respect. ²³They keep you safe from defeat and disaster and from stumbling off the trail. ²⁴⁻²⁶With them on guard you can sleep without fear; you need not be afraid of disaster or the plots of wicked men, for the Lord is with you; he protects you.

²⁷⁻²⁸Don't withhold repayment of your debts. Don't say "some other time," if you can pay now. ²⁹Don't plot against your neighbor; he is trusting you. ³⁰Don't get into needless fights. ³¹Don't envy violent men. Don't copy their ways. ³²For such men are an abomination to the Lord, but he gives his friendship to the godly.

33The curse of God is on the wicked, but his blessing is on the upright. 34The Lord mocks at mockers, but helps the humble. 35The wise are promoted to honor, but fools are promoted to shame!

4 Young men, listen to me as you would to your father. Listen, and grow wise, for I speak the truth—don't turn away. 3For I, too, was once a son, tenderly loved by my mother as an only child, and the companion of my father. 4He told me never to forget his words. "If you follow them," he said, "you will have a long and happy life. 5Learn to be wise," he said, "and develop good judgment and common sense! I cannot overemphasize this point." 6Cling to wisdom—she will protect you. Love her—she will guard you.

7Getting wisdom is the most important thing you can do! And with your wisdom, develop common sense and good judgment. 8-9If you exalt wisdom, she will exalt you. Hold her fast and she will lead you to great honor; she will place a beautiful crown upon your head. 10My son, listen to me and do as I say, and you will have a long, good life.

11I would have you learn this great fact: that a life of doing right is the wisest life there is. 12If you live that kind of life, you'll not limp or stumble as you run. 13Carry out my instructions; don't forget them, for they will lead you to real living.

14Don't do as the wicked do. 15Avoid their haunts—turn away, go somewhere else, 16for evil men can't sleep until they've done their evil deed for the day. They can't rest unless they cause someone to stumble and fall. 17They eat and drink wickedness and violence!

18But the good man walks along in the ever-brightening light of God's favor; the dawn gives way to morning splendor, 19while the evil man gropes and stumbles in the dark.

264

²⁰Listen, son of mine, to what I say. Listen carefully. ²¹Keep these thoughts ever in mind; let them penetrate deep within your heart, ²²for they will mean real life for you, and radiant health.

²³Above all else, guard your affections. For they influence everything else in your life. ²⁴Spurn the careless kiss of a prostitute. Stay far from her. ²⁵Look straight ahead; don't even turn your head to look. ²⁶Watch your step. Stick to the path and be safe. ²⁷Don't sidetrack; pull back your foot from danger.

5 Listen to me, my son! I know what I am saying; listen! ²Watch yourself, lest you be indiscreet and betray some vital information. ³For the lips of a prostitute are as sweet as honey, and smooth flattery is her stock in trade. ⁴But afterwards only a bitter conscience is left to you, sharp as a double-edged sword. ⁵She leads you down to death and hell. ⁶For she does not know the path to life. She staggers down a crooked trail, and doesn't even realize where it leads.

⁷Young men, listen to me, and never forget what I'm about to say: ⁸Run from her! Don't go near her house, ⁹lest you fall to her temptation and lose your honor, and give the remainder of your life to the cruel and merciless; ¹⁰lest strangers obtain your wealth, and you become a slave of foreigners. ¹¹Lest afterwards you groan in anguish and in shame, when syphilis consumes your body, ¹²and you say, "Oh, if only I had listened! If only I had not demanded my own way! ¹³Oh, why wouldn't I take advice? Why was I so stupid? ¹⁴For now I must face public disgrace."

¹⁵Drink from your own well, my son—be faithful and true to your wife. ¹⁶Why should you beget children with women of the street? ¹⁷Why share your children with those outside your home? ¹⁸Be happy, yes, rejoice in the wife of your youth. ¹⁹Let her breasts and tender embrace satisfy you. Let her love alone fill you with delight. ²⁰Why delight yourself with prostitutes, embracing what isn't yours? ²¹For God is closely watching you, and he weighs carefully everything you do.

²²The wicked man is doomed by his own sins; they are ropes that catch and hold him. ²³He shall die because he will not listen to the truth; he has let himself be led away into incredible folly.

6 Son, if you endorse a note for someone you hardly know, guaranteeing his debt, you are in serious trouble. [2]You may have trapped yourself by your agreement. [3]Quick! Get out of it if you possibly can! Swallow your pride; don't let embarrassment stand in the way. Go and beg to have your name erased. [4]Don't put it off. Do it now. Don't rest until you do. [5]If you can get out of this trap you have saved yourself like a deer that escapes from a hunter, or a bird from the net.

⁶Take a lesson from the ants, you lazy fellow. Learn from their ways and be wise! ⁷For though they have no king to make them work, ⁸yet they labor hard all summer, gathering

food for the winter. ⁹But you—all you do is sleep. When will you wake up? ¹⁰"Let me sleep a little longer!" Sure, just a little more! ¹¹And as you sleep, poverty creeps upon you like a robber and destroys you; want attacks you in full armor.

¹²⁻¹³Let me describe for you a worthless and a wicked

man; first, he is a constant liar; he signals his true intentions to his friends with eyes and feet and fingers. ¹⁴He is always thinking up new schemes to swindle people. He stirs up trouble everywhere. ¹⁵But he will be destroyed suddenly, broken beyond hope of healing. ¹⁶⁻¹⁹For there are six things the Lord hates—no, seven: haughtiness, lying, murdering, plotting evil, eagerness to do wrong, a false witness, and sowing discord among brothers.

²⁰Young man, obey your father and your mother. ²¹Take to heart all of their advice; keep in mind everything they tell you. ²²Every day and all night long their counsel will lead you and save you from harm; when you wake up in the morning, let their instructions guide you into the new day. ²³For their advice is a beam of light directed into the dark corners of your mind to warn you of danger and to give you a good life. ²⁴Their counsel will keep you far away from prostitutes with all their flatteries, and unfaithful wives of other men.

²⁵Don't lust for their beauty. Don't let their coyness seduce you. ²⁶For a prostitute will bring a man to poverty, and an adulteress may cost him his very life. ²⁷Can a man hold fire against his chest and not be burned? ²⁸Can he walk on hot coals and not blister his feet? ²⁹So it is with the man who commits adultery with another's wife. He shall not go unpunished for this sin. ³⁰Excuses might even be found for a thief, if he steals when he is starving! ³¹But even so, he is fined seven times as much as he stole, though it may mean selling everything in his house to pay it back.

³²But the man who commits adultery is an utter fool, for he destroys his own soul. ³³Wounds and constant disgrace are his lot, ³⁴for the woman's husband will be furious in his jealousy, and he will have no mercy on you in his day of vengeance. ³⁵You won't be able to buy him off no matter what you offer.

7 Follow my advice, my son; always keep it in mind and stick to it. ²Obey me and live! Guard my words as your most precious possession. ³Write them down, and also keep them deep within your heart. ⁴Love wisdom like a sweetheart; make her a beloved member of your family. ⁵Let her hold you back from affairs with other women—from listening to their flattery.

⁶I was looking out the window of my house one day, ⁷and

saw a simple-minded lad, a young man lacking common sense, [8-9]walking at twilight down the street to the house of this wayward girl, a prostitute. [10]She approached him, saucy and pert, and dressed seductively. [11-12]She was the brash, coarse type, seen often in the streets and markets, soliciting at every corner for men to be her lovers.

[13]She put her arms around him and kissed him, and with a saucy look she said, "I was just coming to look for you and here you are! [14-17]Come home with me and I'll fix you a wonderful dinner, and after that—well, my bed is spread with lovely, colored sheets of finest linen imported from Egypt, perfumed with myrrh, aloes and cinnamon. [18]Come on, let's take our fill of love until morning, [19]for my husband is away on a long trip. [20]He has taken a wallet full of money with him, and won't return for several days."

[21]So she seduced him with her pretty speech, her coaxing and her wheedling, until he yielded to her. He couldn't resist her flattery. [22]He followed her as an ox going to the butcher, or as a stag that is trapped, [23]waiting to be killed with an arrow through its heart. He was as a bird flying into a snare, not knowing the fate awaiting it there.

[24]Listen to me, young men, and not only listen but obey; [25]don't let your desires get out of hand; don't let yourself think about her. Don't go near her; stay away from where she walks, lest she tempt you and seduce you. [26]For she has been the ruin of multitudes—a vast host of men have been her victims. [27]If you want to find the road to hell, look for her house.

8 Can't you hear the voice of wisdom? She is standing at the city gates and at every fork in the road, and at the door of every house. Listen to what she says: [2-5]"Listen, men!" she calls. "How foolish and naive you are! Let me give you understanding. O foolish ones, let me show you common sense! ⁶⁻⁷Listen to me! For I have important information for you. Everything I say is right and true, for I hate lies and every kind of deception. ⁸My advice is wholesome and good. There is nothing of evil in it. ⁹My words are plain and clear to anyone with half a mind—if it is only open! ¹⁰My instruction is far more valuable than silver or gold."

¹¹For the value of wisdom is far above rubies; nothing can be compared with it. ¹²Wisdom and good judgment live together, for wisdom knows where to discover knowledge and understanding. ¹³If anyone respects and fears God, he will hate evil. For wisdom hates pride, arrogance, corruption and deceit of every kind.

¹⁴⁻¹⁶"I, Wisdom, give good advice and common sense. Because of my strength, kings reign in power, and rulers make just laws. ¹⁷I love all who love me. Those who search for me shall surely find me. ¹⁸Unending riches, honor, justice and righteousness are mine to distribute. ¹⁹My gifts are better than the purest gold or sterling silver! ²⁰My paths are those of justice and right. ²¹Those who love and follow me are indeed wealthy. I fill their treasuries. ²²The Lord formed me in the beginning, before he created anything else. ²³From ages past, I am. I existed before the earth began. ²⁴I lived before the oceans were created, before the springs bubbled forth their waters onto the earth; ²⁵before the mountains and the hills were made. ²⁶Yes, I was born before God made the earth and fields, and the first handfuls of soil.

²⁷⁻²⁹"I was there when he established the heavens and formed the great springs in the depths of the oceans. I was there when he set the limits of the seas and gave them his instructions not to spread beyond their boundaries. I was there when he made the blueprint for the earth and oceans.
272

³⁰I was the craftsman at his side. I was his constant delight, rejoicing always in his presence. ³¹And how happy I was with what he created—his wide world and all his family of mankind! ³²And so, young men, listen to me, for how happy are all who follow my instructions.

³³"Listen to my counsel—oh, don't refuse it—and be wise. ³⁴Happy is the man who is so anxious to be with me that he watches for me daily at my gates, or waits for me outside my home! ³⁵For whoever finds me finds life and wins approval from the Lord. ³⁶But the one who misses me has injured himself irreparably. Those who refuse me show that they love death."

9 Wisdom has built a palace supported on seven pillars, ²and has prepared a great banquet, and mixed the wines, ³and sent out her maidens inviting all to come. She calls from the busiest intersections in the city, ⁴"Come, you simple ones without good judgment; ⁵come to wisdom's banquet and drink the wines that I have mixed. ⁶Leave behind your foolishness and begin to live; learn how to be wise."

⁷⁻⁸If you rebuke a mocker, you will only get a smart retort; yes, he will snarl at you. So don't bother with him; he will only hate you for trying to help him. But a wise man, when rebuked, will love you all the more. ⁹Teach a wise man, and he will be the wiser; teach a good man, and he will learn more. ¹⁰For the reverence and fear of God are basic to all wisdom. Knowing God results in every other kind of understanding. ¹¹"I, Wisdom, will make the hours of your day more profitable and the years of your life more fruitful."

¹²Wisdom is its own reward, and if you scorn her, you hurt only yourself.

¹³A prostitute is loud and brash, and never has enough of lust and shame. ¹⁴She sits at the door of her house or stands at the street corners of the city, ¹⁵whispering to men going by, and to those minding their own business. ¹⁶"Come home with me," she urges simpletons. ¹⁷"Stolen melons are the sweetest; stolen apples taste the best!" ¹⁸But they don't realize that her former guests are now citizens of hell.

10 Happy is the man with a level-headed son; sad the mother of a rebel. ²Ill-gotten gain brings no lasting happiness; right living does.

³The Lord will not let a good man starve to death, nor will he let the wicked man's riches continue forever.

⁴Lazy men are soon poor; hard workers get rich.

⁵A wise youth makes hay while the sun shines, but what a shame to see a lad who sleeps away his hour of opportunity.

⁶The good man is covered with blessings from head to foot, but an evil man inwardly curses his luck.

⁷We all have happy memories of good men gone to their reward, but the names of wicked men stink after them.

⁸The wise man is glad to be instructed, but a self-sufficient fool falls flat on his face.

⁹A good man has firm footing, but a crook will slip and fall.

¹⁰Winking at sin leads to sorrow; bold reproof leads to peace.

¹¹There is living truth in what a good man says, but the mouth of the evil man is filled with curses.

¹²Hatred stirs old quarrels, but love overlooks insults.

¹³Men with common sense are admired as counselors; those without it are beaten as servants.

¹⁴A wise man holds his tongue. Only a fool blurts out everything he knows; that only leads to sorrow and trouble.

¹⁵The rich man's wealth is his only strength. The poor man's poverty is his only curse.

¹⁶The good man's earnings advance the cause of righteousness. The evil man squanders his on sin.

¹⁷Anyone willing to be corrected is on the pathway to life. Anyone refusing has lost his chance.

¹⁸To hide hatred is to be a liar; to slander is to be a fool.

¹⁹Don't talk so much. You keep putting your foot in your mouth. Be sensible and turn off the flow!

²⁰When a good man speaks, he is worth listening to, but the words of fools are a dime a dozen.

[21]A godly man gives good advice, but a rebel is destroyed by lack of common sense.

[22]The Lord's blessing is our greatest wealth. All our work adds nothing to it!

[23]A fool's fun is being bad; a wise man's fun is being wise!

[24]The wicked man's fears will all come true, and so will the good man's hopes.

[25]Disaster strikes like a cyclone and the wicked are whirled away. But the good man has a strong anchor.

[26]A lazy fellow is a pain to his employers—like smoke in their eyes or vinegar that sets the teeth on edge.

[27]Reverence for God adds hours to each day; so how can the wicked expect a long, good life?

[28]The hope of good men is eternal happiness; the hopes of evil men are all in vain.

[29]God protects the upright but destroys the wicked.

[30]The good shall never lose God's blessings, but the wicked shall lose everything.

[31]The good man gives wise advice, but the liar's counsel is shunned.

[32]The upright speak what is helpful; the wicked speak rebellion.

11 The Lord hates cheating and delights in honesty. [2]Proud men end in shame, but the meek become wise.

[3]A good man is guided by his honesty; the evil man is destroyed by his dishonesty.

[4]Your riches won't help you on Judgment Day; only righteousness counts then.

[5]Good people are directed by their honesty; the wicked shall fall beneath their load of sins.

⁶The good man's goodness delivers him; the evil man's treachery is his undoing.

⁷When an evil man dies, his hopes all perish, for they are based upon this earthly life.

⁸God rescues good men from danger while letting the wicked fall into it.

⁹Evil words destroy. Godly skill rebuilds.

¹⁰The whole city celebrates a good man's success—and also the godless man's death.

¹¹The good influence of godly citizens causes a city to prosper, but the moral decay of the wicked drives it downhill.

¹²To quarrel with a neighbor is foolish; a man with good sense holds his tongue.

¹³A gossip goes around spreading rumors, while a trustworthy man tries to quiet them.

¹⁴Without wise leadership, a nation is in trouble; but with good counselors there is safety.

¹⁵Be sure you know a person well before you vouch for his credit! Better refuse than suffer later.

¹⁶Honor goes to kind and gracious women, mere money to cruel men.

¹⁷Your own soul is nourished when you are kind; it is destroyed when you are cruel.

¹⁸The evil man gets rich for the moment, but the good man's reward lasts forever.

¹⁹The good man finds life; the evil man, death.

²⁰The Lord hates the stubborn but delights in those who are good.

²¹You can be very sure the evil man will not go unpunished forever. And you can also be very sure God will rescue the children of the godly.

²²A beautiful woman lacking discretion and modesty is like a fine gold ring in a pig's snout.

²³The good man can look forward to happiness, while the wicked can expect only wrath.

²⁴⁻²⁵It is possible to give away and become richer! It is also possible to hold on too tightly and lose everything. Yes, the liberal man shall be rich! By watering others, he waters himself.

²⁶People curse the man who holds his grain for higher prices, but they bless the man who sells it to them in their time of need.

²⁷If you search for good you will find God's favor; if you search for evil you will find his curse.

²⁸Trust in your money and down you go! Trust in God and flourish as a tree!

²⁹The fool who provokes his family to anger and resentment will finally have nothing worthwhile left. He shall be the servant of a wiser man.

³⁰Godly men are growing a tree that bears life-giving fruit, and all who win souls are wise.

³¹Even the godly shall be rewarded here on earth; how much more the wicked!

12

To learn, you must want to be taught. To refuse reproof is stupid.

²The Lord blesses good men and condemns the wicked.

³Wickedness never brings real success; only the godly have that.

⁴A worthy wife is her husband's joy and crown; the other kind corrodes his strength and tears down everything he does.

⁵A good man's mind is filled with honest thoughts; an evil man's mind is crammed with lies.

⁶The wicked accuse; the godly defend.

⁷The wicked shall perish; the godly shall stand.

⁸Everyone admires a man with good sense, but a man with a warped mind is despised.

⁹It is better to get your hands dirty—and eat, than to be too proud to work—and starve.

¹⁰A good man is concerned for the welfare of his animals, but even the kindness of godless men is cruel.

¹¹Hard work means prosperity; only a fool idles away his time.

¹²Crooks are jealous of each other's loot, while good men long to help each other.

¹³Lies will get any man into trouble, but honesty is its own defense.

¹⁴Telling the truth gives a man great satisfaction, and hard work returns many blessings to him.

¹⁵A fool thinks he needs no advice, but a wise man listens to others.

¹⁶A fool is quick-tempered; a wise man stays cool when insulted.

¹⁷A good man is known by his truthfulness; a false man by deceit and lies.

¹⁸Some people like to make cutting remarks, but the

words of the wise soothe and heal.

¹⁹Truth stands the test of time; lies are soon exposed.

²⁰Deceit fills hearts that are plotting for evil; joy fills hearts that are planning for good!

²¹No real harm befalls the good, but there is constant trouble for the wicked.

²²God delights in those who keep their promises, and abhors those who don't.

²³A wise man doesn't display his knowledge, but a fool displays his foolishness.

²⁴Work hard and become a leader; be lazy and never succeed.

²⁵Anxious hearts are very heavy but a word of encouragement does wonders!

²⁶The good man asks advice from friends; the wicked plunge ahead—and fall.

²⁷A lazy man won't even dress the game he gets while hunting, but the diligent man makes good use of everything he finds.

²⁸The path of the godly leads to life. So why fear death?

13

A wise youth accepts his father's rebuke; a young mocker doesn't.

²The good man wins his case by careful argument; the evil-minded only wants to fight.

³Self-control means controlling the tongue! A quick retort can ruin everything.

⁴Lazy people want much but get little, while the diligent are prospering.

⁵A good man hates lies; wicked men lie constantly and come to shame.

⁶A man's goodness helps him all through life, while evil men are being destroyed by their wickedness.

⁷Some rich people are poor, and some poor people have great wealth!

⁸Being kidnapped and held for ransom never worries the poor man!

⁹The good man's life is full of light. The sinner's road is dark and gloomy.

¹⁰Pride leads to arguments; be humble, take advice and become wise.

¹¹Wealth from gambling quickly disappears; wealth from hard work grows.

¹²Hope deferred makes the heart sick; but when dreams come true at last, there is life and joy.

¹³Despise God's Word and find yourself in trouble. Obey it and succeed.

¹⁴The advice of a wise man refreshes like water from a mountain spring. Those accepting it become aware of the pitfalls on ahead.

¹⁵A man with good sense is appreciated. A treacherous man must walk a rocky road.

¹⁶A wise man thinks ahead; a fool doesn't, and even brags about it!

¹⁷An unreliable messenger can cause a lot of trouble.

Reliable communication permits progress.

¹⁸If you refuse criticism you will end in poverty and disgrace; if you accept criticism you are on the road to fame.

¹⁹It is pleasant to see plans develop. That is why fools refuse to give them up even when they are wrong.

²⁰Be with wise men and become wise. Be with evil men and become evil.

²¹Curses chase sinners, while blessings chase the righteous!

²²When a good man dies, he leaves an inheritance to his grandchildren; but when a sinner dies, his wealth is stored up for the godly.

²³A poor man's farm may have good soil, but injustice robs him of its riches.

²⁴If you refuse to discipline your son, it proves you don't love him; for if you love him you will be prompt to punish him.

²⁵The good man eats to live, while the evil man lives to eat.

14

A wise woman builds her house, while a foolish woman tears hers down by her own efforts.

²To do right honors God; to sin is to despise him.

³A rebel's foolish talk should prick his own pride! But the wise man's speech is respected.

⁴An empty stable stays clean—but there is no income from an empty stable.

⁵A truthful witness never lies; a false witness always lies.

⁶A mocker never finds the wisdom he claims he is looking for, yet it comes easily to the man with common sense.

⁷If you are looking for advice, stay away from fools.

⁸The wise man looks ahead. The fool attempts to fool himself and won't face facts.

⁹The common bond of rebels is their guilt. The common bond of godly people is good will.

¹⁰Only the person involved can know his own bitterness or joy—no one else can really share it.

¹¹The work of the wicked will perish; the work of the godly will flourish.

¹²Before every man there lies a wide and pleasant road that seems right but ends in death.

¹³Laughter cannot mask a heavy heart. When the laughter ends, the grief remains.

¹⁴The backslider gets bored with himself; the godly man's life is exciting.

¹⁵Only a simpleton believes everything he's told! A prudent man understands the need for proof.

¹⁶A wise man is cautious and avoids danger; a fool plunges ahead with great confidence.

¹⁷A short-tempered man is a fool. He hates the man who is patient.

¹⁸The simpleton is crowned with folly; the wise man is crowned with knowledge.

¹⁹Evil men shall bow before the godly.

²⁰⁻²¹Even his own neighbors despise the poor man, while the rich have many "friends." But to despise the poor is to sin. Blessed are those who help them.

²²Those who plot evil shall wander away and be lost, but those who plan good shall be granted mercy and quietness.

²³Work brings profit; talk brings poverty!

²⁴Wise men are praised for their wisdom; fools are despised for their folly.

²⁵A witness who tells the truth saves good men from being sentenced to death, but a false witness is a traitor.

²⁶Reverence for God gives a man deep strength; his children have a place of refuge and security.

²⁷Reverence for the Lord is a fountain of life; its waters keep a man from death.

²⁸A growing population is a king's glory; a dwindling nation is his doom.

²⁹A wise man controls his temper. He knows that anger causes mistakes.

³⁰A relaxed attitude lengthens a man's life; jealousy rots it away.

³¹Anyone who oppresses the poor is insulting God who made them. To help the poor is to honor God.

³²The godly have a refuge when they die, but the wicked are crushed by their sins.

³³Wisdom is enshrined in the hearts of men of common sense, but it must shout loudly before fools will hear it.

³⁴Godliness exalts a nation, but sin is a reproach to any people.

³⁵A king rejoices in servants who know what they are doing; he is angry with those who cause trouble.

15 A gentle answer turns away wrath, but harsh words cause quarrels.

²A wise teacher makes learning a joy; a rebellious teacher spouts foolishness.

³The Lord is watching everywhere and keeps his eye on both the evil and the good.

⁴Gentle words cause life and health; griping brings discouragement.

⁵Only a fool despises his father's advice; a wise son considers each suggestion.

⁶There is treasure in being good, but trouble dogs the wicked.

⁷Only the good can give good advice. Rebels can't.

⁸The Lord hates the gifts of the wicked, but delights in the prayers of his people.

⁹⁻¹⁰The Lord despises the deeds of the wicked, but loves

those who try to be good. If they stop trying, the Lord will punish them; if they rebel against that punishment, they will die.

¹¹The depths of hell are open to God's knowledge. How much more the hearts of all mankind!

¹²A mocker stays away from wise men because he hates to be scolded.

¹³A happy face means a glad heart; a sad face means a breaking heart.

¹⁴A wise man is hungry for truth, while the mocker feeds on trash.

¹⁵When a man is gloomy, everything seems to go wrong; when he is cheerful, everything seems right!

¹⁶Better a little with reverence for God, than great treasure and trouble with it.

¹⁷It is better to eat soup with someone you love than steak with someone you hate.

¹⁸A quick-tempered man starts fights; a cool-tempered man tries to stop them.

¹⁹A lazy fellow has trouble all through life; the good man's path is easy!

²⁰A sensible son gladdens his father. A rebellious son saddens his mother.

²¹If a man enjoys folly, something is wrong! The sensible stay on the pathways of right.

²²Plans go wrong with too few counselors; many counselors bring success.

²³Everyone enjoys giving good advice, and how wonderful it is to be able to say the right thing at the right time!

²⁴The road of the godly leads upward, leaving hell behind.

²⁵The Lord destroys the possessions of the proud but cares for widows.

²⁶The Lord hates the thoughts of the wicked but delights in kind words.

²⁷Dishonest money brings grief to all the family, but hating bribes brings happiness.

²⁸A good man thinks before he speaks; the evil man pours out his evil words without a thought.

²⁹The Lord is far from the wicked, but he hears the prayers of the righteous.

³⁰Pleasant sights and good reports give happiness and health.

³¹⁻³²If you profit from constructive criticism you will be elected to the wise men's hall of fame. But to reject criticism is to harm yourself and your own best interests.

³³Humility and reverence for the Lord will make you both wise and honored.

16

We can make our plans, but the final outcome is in God's hands.

²We can always "prove" that we are right, but is the Lord convinced?

³Commit your work to the Lord, then it will succeed.

⁴The Lord has made everything for his own purposes—even the wicked, for punishment.

⁵Pride disgusts the Lord. Take my word for it—proud men shall be punished.

⁶Iniquity is atoned for by mercy and truth; evil is avoided by reverence for God.

⁷When a man is trying to please God, God makes even his worst enemies to be at peace with him.

⁸A little, gained honestly, is better than great wealth gotten by dishonest means.

⁹We should make plans—counting on God to direct us.

¹⁰God will help the king to judge the people fairly; there need be no mistakes.

¹¹The Lord demands fairness in every business deal. He established this principle.

¹²It is a horrible thing for a king to do evil. His right to rule depends upon his fairness.

¹³The king rejoices when his people are truthful and fair.

¹⁴The anger of the king is a messenger of death and a wise man will appease it.

¹⁵Many favors are showered on those who please the king.

¹⁶How much better is wisdom than gold, and understanding than silver!

¹⁷The path of the godly leads away from evil; he who follows that path is safe.

¹⁸Pride goes before destruction and haughtiness before a fall.

¹⁹Better poor and humble than proud and rich.

²⁰God blesses those who obey him; happy the man who puts his trust in the Lord.

²¹The wise man is known by his common sense, and a pleasant teacher is the best.

²²Wisdom is a fountain of life to those possessing it, but a fool's burden is his folly.

²³From a wise mind comes careful and persuasive speech.

²⁴Kind words are like honey—enjoyable and healthful.

²⁵Before every man there lies a wide and pleasant road he thinks is right, but it ends in death.

²⁶Hunger is good—if it makes you work to satisfy it!

²⁷Idle hands are the devil's workshop; idle lips are his mouthpiece.

²⁸An evil man sows strife; gossip separates the best of friends.

²⁹Wickedness loves company—and leads others into sin.

³⁰The wicked man stares into space with pursed lips, deep in thought, planning his evil deeds.

³¹White hair is a crown of glory and is seen most among the godly.

³²It is better to be slow-tempered than famous; it is better to have self-control than to control an army.

³³We toss the coin, but it is the Lord who controls its decision.

17

A dry crust eaten in peace is better than steak every day along with argument and strife. ²A wise slave will rule his master's wicked sons and share their estate.

³Silver and gold are purified by fire, but God purifies hearts.

⁴The wicked enjoy fellowship with others who are wicked; liars enjoy liars.

⁵Mocking the poor is mocking the God who made them. He will punish those who rejoice at others' misfortunes.

⁶An old man's grandchildren are his crowning glory. A child's glory is his father.

⁷Truth from a rebel or lies from a king are both unexpected.

⁸A bribe works like magic. Whoever uses it will prosper!

⁹Love forgets mistakes; nagging about them parts the best of friends.

¹⁰A rebuke to a man of common sense is more effective than a hundred lashes on the back of a rebel.

¹¹The wicked live for rebellion; they shall be severely punished.

¹²It is safer to meet a bear robbed of her cubs than a fool caught in his folly.

¹³If you repay evil for good, a curse is upon your home.

¹⁴It is hard to stop a quarrel once it starts, so don't let it begin.

¹⁵The Lord despises those who say that bad is good, and good is bad.

¹⁶It is senseless to pay tuition to educate a rebel who has no heart for truth.

¹⁷A true friend is always loyal, and a brother is born to help in time of need.

¹⁸It is poor judgment to countersign another's note, to become responsible for his debts.

¹⁹Sinners love to fight; boasting is looking for trouble.

²⁰An evil man is suspicious of everyone and tumbles into constant trouble.

²¹It's no fun to be a rebel's father.

²²A cheerful heart does good like medicine, but a broken spirit makes one sick.

²³It is wrong to accept a bribe to twist justice.

²⁴Wisdom is the main pursuit of sensible men, but a fool's goals are at the ends of the earth!

²⁵A rebellious son is a grief to his father and a bitter blow to his mother.

²⁶How short-sighted to fine the godly for being good! And to punish nobles for being honest!

²⁷⁻²⁸The man of few words and settled mind is wise; therefore, even a fool is thought to be wise when he is silent. It pays him to keep his mouth shut.

18 The selfish man quarrels against every sound principle of conduct by demanding his own way.

²A rebel doesn't care about the facts. All he wants to do is yell.

³Sin brings disgrace.

⁴A wise man's words express deep streams of thought.

⁵It is wrong for a judge to favor the wicked and condemn the innocent.

⁶⁻⁷A fool gets into constant fights. His mouth is his undoing! His words endanger him.

⁸What dainty morsels rumors are. They are eaten with great relish!

⁹A lazy man is brother to the saboteur.

¹⁰The Lord is a strong fortress. The godly run to him and are safe.

¹¹The rich man thinks of his wealth as an impregnable defense, a high wall of safety. What a dreamer!

¹²Pride ends in destruction; humility ends in honor.

¹³What a shame—yes, how stupid!—to decide before

knowing the facts!

¹⁴A man's courage can sustain his broken body, but when courage dies, what hope is left?

¹⁵The intelligent man is always open to new ideas. In fact, he looks for them.

¹⁶A gift does wonders; it will bring you before men of importance!

¹⁷Any story sounds true until someone tells the other side and sets the record straight.

¹⁸A coin toss ends arguments and settles disputes between powerful opponents.

¹⁹It is harder to win back the friendship of an offended brother than to capture a fortified city. His anger shuts you out like iron bars.

²⁰Ability to give wise advice satisfies like a good meal!

²¹Those who love to talk will suffer the consequences. Men have died for saying the wrong thing!

294

²²The man who finds a wife finds a good thing; she is a blessing to him from the Lord.

²³The poor man pleads and the rich man answers with insults.

²⁴There are "friends" who pretend to be friends, but there is a friend who sticks closer than a brother.

19

Better be poor and honest than rich and dishonest.

²It is dangerous and sinful to rush into the unknown.

³A man may ruin his chances by his own foolishness and then blame it on the Lord!

⁴A wealthy man has many "friends"; the poor man has none left.

⁵Punish false witnesses. Track down liars.

⁶Many beg favors from a man who is generous; everyone is his friend!

⁷A poor man's own brothers turn away from him in embarrassment; how much more his friends! He calls after them, but they are gone.

⁸He who loves wisdom loves his own best interest and will be a success.

⁹A false witness shall be punished and a liar shall be caught.

¹⁰It doesn't seem right for a fool to succeed or for a slave to rule over princes!

¹¹A wise man restrains his anger and overlooks insults. This is to his credit.

¹²The king's anger is as dangerous as a lion's. But his approval is as refreshing as the dew on grass.

¹³A rebellious son is a calamity to his father, and a nagging wife annoys like constant dripping.

¹⁴A father can give his sons homes and riches, but only the Lord can give them understanding wives.

¹⁵A lazy man sleeps soundly—and he goes hungry!

¹⁶Keep the commandments and keep your life; despising them means death.

¹⁷When you help the poor you are lending to the Lord— and he pays wonderful interest on your loan!

¹⁸Discipline your son in his early years while there is hope. If you don't you will ruin his life.

¹⁹A short-tempered man must bear his own penalty; you can't do much to help him. If you try once you must try a dozen times!

²⁰Get all the advice you can and be wise the rest of your life.

296

²¹Man proposes, but God disposes.

²²Kindness makes a man attractive. And it is better to be poor than dishonest.

²³Reverence for God gives life, happiness, and protection from harm.

²⁴Some men are so lazy they won't even feed themselves!

²⁵Punish a mocker and others will learn from his example. Reprove a wise man and he will be the wiser.

²⁶A son who mistreats his father or mother is a public disgrace.

²⁷Stop listening to teaching that contradicts what you know is right.

²⁸A worthless witness cares nothing for truth—he enjoys his sinning too much.

²⁹Mockers and rebels shall be severely punished.

20 Wine gives false courage; hard liquor leads to brawls; what fools men are to let it master them, making them reel drunkenly down the street!

²The king's fury is like that of a roaring lion; to rouse his anger is to risk your life.

³It is an honor for a man to stay out of a fight. Only fools insist on quarreling.

⁴If you won't plow in the cold, you won't eat at the harvest.

⁵Though good advice lies deep within a counselor's heart, the wise man will draw it out.

⁶Most people will tell you what loyal friends they are, but are they telling the truth?

⁷It is a wonderful heritage to have an honest father.

⁸A king sitting as judge weighs all the evidence carefully, distinguishing the true from false.

⁹Who can ever say, "I have cleansed my heart; I am sinless"?

¹⁰The Lord despises every kind of cheating.

¹¹The character of even a child can be known by the way he acts—whether what he does is pure and right.

¹²If you have good eyesight and good hearing, thank God who gave them to you.

¹³If you love sleep, you will end in poverty. Stay awake, work hard, and there will be plenty to eat!

¹⁴"Utterly worthless!" says the buyer as he haggles over the price. But afterwards he brags about his bargain!

¹⁵Good sense is far more valuable than gold or precious jewels.

¹⁶It is risky to make loans to strangers!

¹⁷Some men enjoy cheating, but the cake they buy with such ill-gotten gain will turn to gravel in their mouths.

¹⁸Don't go ahead with your plans without the advice of others; don't go to war until they agree.

¹⁹Don't tell your secrets to a gossip unless you want them broadcast to the world.

²⁰God puts out the light of the man who curses his father or mother.

²¹Quick wealth is not a blessing in the end.

²²Don't repay evil for evil. Wait for the Lord to handle the matter.

²³The Lord loathes all cheating and dishonesty.

²⁴Since the Lord is directing our steps, why try to understand everything that happens along the way?

²⁵It is foolish and rash to make a promise to the Lord before counting the cost.

²⁶A wise king stamps out crime by severe punishment.

²⁷A man's conscience is the Lord's searchlight exposing his hidden motives.

²⁸If a king is kind, honest and fair, his kingdom stands secure.

²⁹The glory of young men is their strength; of old men, their experience.

³⁰Punishment that hurts chases evil from the heart.

21 Just as water is turned into irrigation ditches, so the Lord directs the king's thoughts. He turns them wherever he wants to.

²We can justify our every deed but God looks at our motives.

³God is more pleased when we are just and fair than when we give him gifts.

⁴Pride, lust, and evil actions are all sin.

⁵Steady plodding brings prosperity; hasty speculation brings poverty.

⁶Dishonest gain will never last, so why take the risk?

⁷Because the wicked are unfair, their violence

boomerangs and destroys them.

⁸A man is known by his actions. An evil man lives an evil life; a good man lives a godly life.

⁹It is better to live in the corner of an attic than with a crabby woman in a lovely home.

¹⁰An evil man loves to harm others; being a good neighbor is out of his line.

¹¹The wise man learns by listening; the simpleton can learn only by seeing scorners punished.

¹²God, the Righteous One, knows what is going on in the homes of the wicked, and will bring the wicked to judgment.

¹³He who shuts his ears to the cries of the poor will be ignored in his own time of need.

¹⁴An angry man is silenced by giving him a gift!

¹⁵A good man loves justice, but it is a calamity to evildoers.

¹⁶The man who strays away from common sense will end up dead!

¹⁷A man who loves pleasure becomes poor; wine and luxury are not the way to riches!

¹⁸The wicked will finally lose; the righteous will finally win.

¹⁹Better to live in the desert than with a quarrelsome, complaining woman.

²⁰The wise man saves for the future, but the foolish man spends whatever he gets.

²¹The man who tries to be good, loving and kind finds life, righteousness and honor.

²²The wise man conquers the strong man and levels his defenses.

²³Keep your mouth closed and you'll stay out of trouble.

²⁴Mockers are proud, haughty and arrogant.

²⁵⁻²⁶The lazy man longs for many things but his hands refuse to work. He is greedy to get,

while the godly love to give!

²⁷God loathes the gifts of evil men, especially if they are trying to bribe him!

²⁸No one believes a liar, but everyone respects the words of an honest man.

²⁹An evil man is stubborn, but a godly man will reconsider.

³⁰No one, regardless of how shrewd or well-advised he is, can stand against the Lord.

³¹Go ahead and prepare for the conflict, but victory comes from God.

22

If you must choose, take a good name rather than great riches; for to be held in loving esteem is better than silver and gold.

²The rich and the poor are alike before the Lord who made them all.

³A prudent man foresees the difficulties ahead and prepares for them; the simpleton goes blindly on and suffers the consequences.

⁴True humility and respect for the Lord lead a man to riches, honor and long life.

⁵The rebel walks a thorny, treacherous road; the man who values his soul will stay away.

⁶Teach a child to choose the right path, and when he is older he will remain upon it.

⁷Just as the rich rule the poor, so the borrower is servant to the lender.

⁸The unjust tyrant will reap disaster and his reign of terror shall end.

⁹Happy is the generous man, the one who feeds the poor.

¹⁰Throw out the mocker, and you will be rid of tension, fighting and quarrels.

¹¹He who values grace and truth is the king's friend.

¹²The Lord preserves the upright but ruins the plans of the wicked.

¹³The lazy man is full of excuses. "I can't go to work!" he says. "If I go outside I might meet a lion in the street and be killed!"

¹⁴A prostitute is a dangerous trap; those cursed of God are caught in it.

¹⁵A youngster's heart is filled with rebellion, but punishment will drive it out of him.

¹⁶He who gains by oppressing the poor or by bribing the rich shall end in poverty.

¹⁷⁻¹⁹Listen to this wise advice; follow it closely, for it will do you good, and you can pass it on to others: Trust in the Lord.

²⁰⁻²¹In the past, haven't I been right? Then believe what I am telling you now, and share it with others.

²²⁻²³Don't rob the poor and sick! For the Lord is their defender. If you injure them he will punish you.

²⁴⁻²⁵Keep away from angry, short-tempered men, lest you learn to be like them and endanger your soul.

²⁶⁻²⁷Unless you have the extra cash on hand, don't countersign a note. Why risk everything you own? They'll even take your bed!

²⁸Do not move the ancient boundary marks. That is stealing.

²⁹Do you know a hard-working man? He shall be successful and stand before kings!

23 When dining with a rich man, be on your guard and don't stuff yourself, though it all tastes so good; for he is trying to bribe you, and no good is going to come of his invitation.

²⁻⁵Don't weary yourself trying to get rich. Why waste your time? For riches can disappear as though they had the wings of a bird!

⁶⁻⁸Don't associate with evil men; don't long for their favors and gifts. Their kindness is a trick; they want to use you as their pawn. The delicious food they serve will turn sour in your stomach and you will vomit it, and have to take back your words of appreciation for their "kindness."

⁹Don't waste your breath on a rebel. He will despise the wisest advice.

¹⁰⁻¹¹Don't steal the land of defenseless orphans by moving their ancient boundary marks, for their Redeemer is strong; he himself will accuse you.

¹²Don't refuse to accept criticism; get all the help you can.

¹³⁻¹⁴Don't fail to correct your children; discipline won't hurt them! They won't die if you use a stick on them! Punishment will keep them out of hell.

¹⁵⁻¹⁶My son, how I will rejoice if you become a man of common sense. Yes, my heart will thrill to your thoughtful, wise words.

¹⁷⁻¹⁸Don't envy evil men but continue to reverence the Lord all the time, for surely you have a wonderful future ahead of you. There is hope for you yet!

¹⁹⁻²¹O my son, be wise and stay in God's paths; don't carouse with drunkards and gluttons, for they are on their way to poverty. And remember that too much sleep clothes a man with rags. ²²Listen to your father's advice and don't despise an old mother's experience. ²³Get the facts at any price, and hold on tightly to all the good sense you can get.

²⁴⁻²⁵The father of a godly man has cause for joy—what pleasure a wise son is! So give your parents joy!

²⁶⁻²⁸O my son, trust my advice—stay away from prostitutes. For a prostitute is a deep and narrow grave. Like a robber, she waits for her victims as one after another become unfaithful to their wives.

²⁹⁻³⁰Whose heart is filled with anguish and sorrow? Who is always fighting and quarreling? Who is the man with bloodshot eyes and many wounds? It is the one who spends long hours in the taverns, trying out new mixtures. ³¹Don't let the sparkle and the smooth taste of strong wine deceive you. ³²For in the end it bites like a poisonous serpent; it stings like an adder. ³³You will see hallucinations and have delirium tremens, and you will say foolish, silly things that would embarrass you no end when sober. ³⁴You will stagger like a sailor tossed at sea, clinging to a swaying mast. ³⁵And afterwards you will say, "I didn't even know it when they beat me up. Let's go and have another drink!"

24

Don't envy godless men; don't even enjoy their company.

²For they spend their days plotting violence and cheating.

³⁻⁴Any enterprise is built by wise planning, becomes strong through common sense, and profits wonderfully by keeping abreast of the facts.

⁵A wise man is mightier than a strong man. Wisdom is mightier than strength.

⁶Don't go to war without wise guidance; there is safety in many counselors.

⁷Wisdom is too much for a rebel. He'll not be chosen as a counselor!

⁸To plan evil is as wrong as doing it.

⁹The rebel's schemes are sinful, and the mocker is the scourge of all mankind.

¹⁰You are a poor specimen if you can't stand the pressure of adversity.

¹¹⁻¹²Rescue those who are unjustly sentenced to death; don't stand back and let them die. Don't try to disclaim responsibility by saying you didn't know about it. For God, who knows all hearts, knows yours, and he knows you knew! And he will reward everyone according to his deeds.

¹³⁻¹⁴My son, honey whets the appetite, and so does wisdom! When you enjoy becoming wise, there is hope for you! A bright future lies ahead!

¹⁵⁻¹⁶O evil man, leave the upright man alone, and quit trying to cheat him out of his rights. Don't you know that this good man, though you trip him up seven times, will each time rise again? But one calamity is enough to lay you low.

¹⁷Do not rejoice when your enemy meets trouble. Let there be no gladness when he falls:

¹⁸for the Lord may be displeased with you and stop punishing him!

¹⁹⁻²⁰Don't envy the wicked. Don't covet his riches. For the evil man has no future; his light will be snuffed out.

²¹⁻²²My son, watch your step before the Lord and the king, and don't associate with radicals. For you will go down with them to sudden disaster, and who knows where it all will end?

²³It is wrong to sentence the poor, and let the rich go free.

²⁴He who says to the wicked, "You are innocent," shall be cursed by many people of many nations;

²⁵but blessings shall be showered on those who rebuke sin fearlessly.

²⁶It is an honor to receive a frank reply.

²⁷Develop your business first before building your house.

²⁸⁻²⁹Don't testify spitefully against an innocent neighbor. Why lie about him? Don't say, "Now I can pay him back for all his meanness to me!"

³⁰⁻³¹I walked by the field of a certain lazy fellow and saw that it was overgrown with thorns, and covered with weeds; and its walls were broken down. ³²⁻³³Then, as I looked, I learned this lesson: "A little extra sleep, a little more slumber, a little folding of the hands to rest" ³⁴means that poverty will break in upon you suddenly like a robber, and violently like a bandit.

25

These proverbs of Solomon were discovered and copied by the aides of King Hezekiah of Judah:

²⁻³It is God's privilege to conceal things, and the king's privilege to discover and invent. You cannot understand the height of heaven, the size of the earth, or all that goes on in the king's mind!

⁴⁻⁵When you remove dross from silver, you have sterling ready for the silversmith. When you remove corrupt men from the king's court, his reign will be just and fair.

⁶⁻⁷Don't demand an audience with the king as though you were some powerful prince. It is better to wait for an invitation rather than to be sent back to the end of the line, publicly disgraced!

⁸⁻¹⁰Don't be hot-headed and rush to court! You may start something you can't finish and go down before your neighbor in shameful defeat. So discuss the matter with him privately. Don't tell anyone else, lest he accuse you of slander and you can't withdraw what you said.

¹¹Timely advice is as lovely as gold apples in a silver basket.

¹²It is a badge of honor to accept valid criticism.

¹³A faithful employee is as refreshing as a cool day in the hot summertime.

¹⁴One who doesn't give the gift he promised is like a cloud blowing over a desert without dropping any rain.

¹⁵Be patient and you will finally win, for a soft tongue can break hard bones.

¹⁶Do you like honey? Don't eat too much of it, or it will make you sick!

¹⁷Don't visit your neighbor too often, or you will outwear your welcome!.

¹⁸Telling lies about someone is as harmful as hitting him with an axe, or wounding him with a sword, or shooting him with a sharp arrow.

¹⁹Putting confidence in an unreliable man is like chewing with a sore tooth, or trying to run on a broken foot.

²⁰Being happy-go-lucky around a person whose heart is heavy is as bad as stealing his jacket in cold weather, or rubbing salt in his wounds.

²¹⁻²²If your enemy is hungry, give him food! If he is thirsty, give him something to drink! This will make him feel ashamed of himself, and God will reward you.

²³As surely as a wind from the north brings cold, just as surely a retort causes anger!

²⁴It is better to live in a corner of an attic than in a beautiful home with a cranky, quarrelsome woman.

²⁵Good news from far away is like cold water to the thirsty.

²⁶If a godly man compromises with the wicked, it is like polluting a fountain or muddying a spring.

²⁷Just as it is harmful to eat too much honey, so also it is bad for men to think about all the honors they deserve!

²⁸A man without self-control is as defenseless as a city with broken-down walls.

26

Honor doesn't go with fools any more than snow with summertime or rain with harvest time!

²An undeserved curse has no effect. Its intended victim will be no more harmed by it than by a sparrow or swallow flitting through the sky.

³Guide a horse with a whip, a donkey with a bridle, and a rebel with a rod to his back!

⁴⁻⁵When arguing with a rebel, don't use foolish arguments as he does, or you will become as foolish as he is! Prick his conceit with silly replies!

⁶To trust a rebel to convey a message is as foolish as cutting off your feet and drinking poison!

⁷In the mouth of a fool a proverb becomes as useless as a paralyzed leg.

⁸Honoring a rebel will backfire like a stone tied to a slingshot!

⁹A rebel will misapply an illustration so that its point will no more be felt than a thorn in the hand of a drunkard.

¹⁰The master may get better work from an untrained apprentice than from a skilled rebel!

¹¹As a dog returns to his vomit, so a fool repeats his folly.

¹²There is one thing worse than a fool, and that is a man who is conceited.

¹³The lazy man won't go out and work. "There might be a lion outside!" he says.

¹⁴He sticks to his bed like a door to its hinges!

¹⁵He is too tired even to lift his food from his dish to his mouth!

¹⁶Yet in his own opinion he is smarter than seven wise men.

¹⁷Yanking a dog's ears is no more foolish than interfering in an argument that isn't any of your business.

¹⁸⁻¹⁹A man who is caught lying to his neighbor and says, "I was just fooling," is like a madman throwing around firebrands, arrows and death!

²⁰Fire goes out for lack of fuel, and tensions disappear when gossip stops.

²¹A quarrelsome man starts fights as easily as a match sets fire to paper.

²²Gossip is a dainty morsel eaten with great relish.

²³Pretty words may hide a wicked heart, just as a pretty glaze covers a common clay pot.

²⁴⁻²⁶A man with hate in his heart may sound pleasant enough, but don't believe him; for he is cursing you in his heart. Though he pretends to be so kind, his hatred will finally come to light for all to see.

²⁷The man who sets a trap for others will get caught in it himself. Roll a boulder down on someone, and it will roll back and crush you.

²⁸Flattery is a form of hatred and wounds cruelly.

27

Don't brag about your plans for tomorrow—wait and see what happens.

²Don't praise yourself; let others do it!

³A rebel's frustrations are heavier than sand and rocks.

⁴Jealousy is more dangerous and cruel than anger.

⁵Open rebuke is better than hidden love!

⁶Wounds from a friend are better than kisses from an enemy!

⁷Even honey seems tasteless to a man who is full; but if he is hungry, he'll eat anything!

⁸A man who strays from home is like a bird that wanders from its nest.

⁹Friendly suggestions are as pleasant as perfume.

¹⁰Never abandon a friend—either yours or your father's. Then you won't need to go to a distant relative for help in your time of need.

¹¹My son, how happy I will be if you turn out to be sensible! It will be a public honor to me.

¹²A sensible man watches for problems ahead and prepares to meet them. The simpleton never looks, and suffers the consequences.

¹³The world's poorest credit risk is the man who agrees to pay a stranger's debts.

¹⁴If you shout a pleasant greeting to a friend too early in the morning, he will count it as a curse!

¹⁵A constant dripping on a rainy day and a cranky woman are much alike!

¹⁶You can no more stop her complaints than you can stop the wind or hold onto anything with oil-slick hands.

¹⁷A friendly discussion is as stimulating as the sparks that fly when iron strikes iron.

¹⁸A workman may eat from the orchard he tends; anyone should be rewarded who protects another's interests.

¹⁹A mirror reflects a man's face, but what he is really like is

shown by the kind of friends he chooses.

²⁰Ambition and death are alike in this: neither is ever satisfied.

²¹The purity of silver and gold can be tested in a crucible, but a man is tested by his reaction to men's praise.

²²You can't separate a rebel from his foolishness though you crush him to powder.

²³⁻²⁴Riches can disappear fast. And the king's crown doesn't stay in his family forever—so watch your business interests closely. Know the state of your flocks and your herds; ²⁵⁻²⁷then there will be lamb's wool enough for clothing, and goat's milk enough for food for all your household after the hay is harvested, and the new crop appears, and the mountain grasses are gathered in.

28 The wicked flee when no one is chasing them! But the godly are bold as lions!

²When there is moral rot within a nation, its government topples easily; but with honest, sensible leaders there is stability.

³When a poor man oppresses those even poorer, he is like an unexpected flood sweeping away their last hope.

⁴To complain about the law is to praise wickedness. To obey the law is to fight evil.

⁵Evil men don't understand the importance of justice, but those who follow the Lord are much concerned about it.

⁶Better to be poor and honest than rich and a cheater.

⁷Young men who are wise obey the law; a son who is a member of a lawless gang is a shame to his father.

⁸Income from exploiting the poor will end up in the hands of someone who pities them.

⁹God doesn't listen to the prayers of those who flout the law.

¹⁰A curse on those who lead astray the godly. But men who encourage the upright to do good shall be given a worthwhile reward.

¹¹Rich men are conceited, but their real poverty is evident

to the poor.

12When the godly are successful, everyone is glad. When the wicked succeed, everyone is sad.

13A man who refuses to admit his mistakes can never be successful. But if he confesses and forsakes them, he gets another chance.

14Blessed is the man who reveres God, but the man who doesn't care is headed for serious trouble.

15A wicked ruler is as dangerous to the poor as a lion or bear attacking them.

16Only a stupid prince will oppress his people, but a king will have a long reign if he hates dishonesty and bribes.

17A murderer's conscience will drive him into hell. Don't stop him!

18Good men will be rescued from harm, but cheaters will be destroyed.

19Hard work brings prosperity; playing around brings poverty.

20The man who wants to do right will get a rich reward. But the man who wants to get rich quick will quickly fail.

21Giving preferred treatment to rich people is a clear case of selling one's soul for a piece of bread.

22Trying to get rich quick is evil and leads to poverty.

23In the end, people appreciate frankness more than flattery.

24A man who robs his parents and says, "What's wrong with that?" is no better than a murderer.

25Greed causes fighting; trusting God leads to prosperity.

26A man is a fool to trust himself! But those who use God's wisdom are safe.

27If you give to the poor, your needs will be supplied! But a curse upon those who close their eyes to poverty.

28When the wicked prosper, good men go away; when the wicked meet disaster, good men return.

29 The man who is often reproved but refuses to accept criticism will suddenly be broken and never have another chance.

²With good men in authority, the people rejoice; but with the wicked in power, they groan.

³A wise son makes his father happy, but a lad who hangs around with prostitutes disgraces him.

⁴A just king gives stability to his nation, but one who demands bribes destroys it.

⁵⁻⁶Flattery is a trap; evil men are caught in it, but good men stay away and sing for joy.

⁷The good man knows the poor man's rights; the godless don't care.

⁸Fools start fights everywhere while wise men try to keep peace.

⁹There's no use arguing with a fool. He only rages and scoffs, and tempers flare.

¹⁰The godly pray for those who long to kill them.

¹¹A rebel shouts in anger; a wise man holds his temper in and cools it.

¹²A wicked ruler will have wicked aides on his staff.

¹³Rich and poor are alike in this: each depends on God for light.

¹⁴A king who is fair to the poor shall have a long reign.

¹⁵Scolding and spanking a child helps him to learn. Left to himself, he brings shame to his mother.

¹⁶When rulers are wicked, their people are too; but good men will live to see the tyrant's downfall.

¹⁷Discipline your son and he will give you happiness and peace of mind.

¹⁸Where there is ignorance of God, crime runs wild; but what a wonderful thing it is for a nation to know and keep his laws.

¹⁹Sometimes mere words are not enough—discipline is

needed. For the words may not be heeded.

²⁰There is more hope for a fool than for a man of quick temper.

²¹Pamper a servant from childhood, and he will expect you to treat him as a son!

²²A hot-tempered man starts fights and gets into all kinds of trouble.

²³Pride ends in a fall, while humility brings honor.

²⁴A man who assists a thief must really hate himself! For he knows the consequence but does it anyway.

²⁵Fear of man is a dangerous trap, but to trust in God means safety.

²⁶Do you want justice? Don't fawn on the judge, but ask the Lord for it!

²⁷The good hate the badness of the wicked. The wicked hate the goodness of the good.

30

These are the messages of Agur, son of Jakeh, addressed to Ithiel and Ucal:

²I am tired out, O God, and ready to die. I am too stupid even to call myself a human being! ³I cannot understand man, let alone God. ⁴Who else but God goes back and forth to heaven? Who else holds the wind in his fists, and wraps up the oceans in his cloak? Who but God has created the world? If there is any other, what is his name—and his Son's name—if you know it?

⁵Every word of God proves true. He defends all who come to him for protection. ⁶Do not add to his words, lest he rebuke you, and you be found a liar.

⁷O God, I beg two favors from you before I die: ⁸First, help me never to tell a lie. Second, give me neither poverty nor riches! Give me just enough to satisfy my needs! ⁹For if I grow rich, I may become content without God. And if I am too poor, I may steal, and thus insult God's holy name.

¹⁰Never falsely accuse a man to his employer, lest he curse you for your sin.

¹¹⁻¹²There are those who curse their father and mother, and feel themselves faultless despite their many sins. ¹³⁻¹⁴They are proud beyond description, arrogant, disdainful. They devour the poor with teeth as sharp as knives!

¹⁵⁻¹⁶There are two things never satisfied, like a leech forever craving more: no, three things! no, four! Hell, the barren womb, a barren desert, fire.

¹⁷A man who mocks his father and despises his mother shall have his eye plucked out by ravens and eaten by vultures. ¹⁸⁻¹⁹There are three things too wonderful for me to understand—no, four! How an eagle glides through the sky. How a serpent crawls upon a rock. How a ship finds its way across the heaving ocean. The growth of love between a man and a girl. ²⁰There is another thing too: how a prostitute can sin and then say, "What's wrong with that?"

²¹⁻²³There are three things that make the earth tremble—no, four it cannot stand: A slave who becomes a king. A rebel who prospers. A bitter woman when she finally marries. A servant girl who marries her mistress' husband.

²⁴⁻²⁸There are four things that are small but unusually wise: Ants: they aren't strong, but store up food for the winter. Cliff badgers: delicate little animals who protect themselves by living among the rocks. The locusts: though they have no leader, they stay together in swarms. The lizards: they are easy to catch and kill, yet are found even in king's palaces!

²⁹⁻³¹There are three stately monarchs in the earth—no, four: The lion, king of the animals. He won't turn aside for anyone. The peacock. The male goat. A king as he leads his army.

³²If you have been a fool by being proud or plotting evil, don't brag about it—cover your mouth with your hand in shame.

³³As the churning of cream yields butter, and a blow to the nose causes bleeding, so anger causes quarrels.

31

These are the wise sayings of King Lemuel of Massa, taught to him at his mother's knee: ²O my son, whom I have dedicated to the Lord, ³do not spend your time with women—the royal pathway to destruction.

⁴And it is not for kings, O Lemuel, to drink wine and whiskey. ⁵For if they drink they may forget their duties and be unable to give justice to those who are oppressed. ⁶⁻⁷Hard liquor is for sick men at the brink of death, and wine for those in deep depression. Let them drink to forget their poverty and misery.

⁸You should defend those who cannot help themselves.

9Yes, speak up for the poor and helpless, and see that they get justice.

10If you can find a truly good wife, she is worth more than precious gems! 11Her husband can trust her, and she will richly satisfy his needs. 12She will not hinder him, but help him all her life. 13She finds wool and flax and busily spins it. 14She buys imported foods, brought by ship from distant ports. 15She gets up before dawn to prepare breakfast for her household, and plans the day's work for her servant girls. 16She goes out to inspect a field, and buys it; with her own hands she plants a vineyard. 17She is energetic, a hard worker, 18and watches for bargains. She works far into the night!

19-20She sews for the poor, and generously helps those in need. 21She has no fear of winter for her household, for she has made warm clothes for all of them. 22She also up-holsters with finest tapestry; her own clothing is beautifully made—a purple gown of pure linen. 23Her husband is well known, for he sits in the council chamber with the other civic leaders. 24She makes belted linen garments to sell to the merchants.

25She is a woman of strength and dignity, and has no fear of old age. 26When she speaks, her words are wise, and kindness is the rule for everything she says. 27She watches carefully all that goes on throughout her household, and is never lazy. 28Her children stand and bless her; so does her husband. He praises her with these words: 29"There are many fine women in the world, but you are the best of them all!"

30Charm can be deceptive and beauty doesn't last, but a woman who fears and reverences God shall be greatly praised. 31Praise her for the many fine things she does. These good deeds of hers shall bring her honor and recognition from people of importance.